MARRIED SAINTS

Visit our website at
WWW.ALBAHOUSE.ORG

Married Saints

JOHN F. FINK

ALBA·HOUSE   NEW·YORK

SOCIETY OF ST. PAUL, 2187 VICTORY BLVD., STATEN ISLAND, NEW YORK 10314

Library of Congress Cataloging-in-Publication Data

Fink, John F.
   Married saints / John F. Fink.
      p. cm.
   ISBN 0-8189-0822-X
   1. Married Christian saints — Biography. 2. Catholic Church —
Biography. I. Title.
BX4661.F55   1999
282'.092'2 — dc21   98-28459
  [B]   CIP

Produced and designed in the United States of America by the
Fathers and Brothers of the Society of St. Paul,
2187 Victory Boulevard, Staten Island, New York 10314,
as part of their communications apostolate.

ISBN: 0-8189-0822-X

Printing Information:

Current Printing - first digit 1 2 3 4 5 6 7 8 9 10

Year of Current Printing - first year shown

1999   2000   2001   2002   2003   2004   2005   2006

TABLE OF CONTENTS

DEDICATION

To Marie,
who has to be a saint
to be married to me since 1955.

INTRODUCTION

When I told people that I was writing a book about married saints, I got some strange reactions. "Are there any?" more than one person asked. "That will be a small book," another said. Others said, "Great! We really need that." One man, married of course, simply started to applaud.

The simple fact is that *most* of the saints were married! Did that statement startle you? It's based on the fact that the overwhelming majority of people do marry and the only qualification for being a saint is that you go to heaven instead of to hell when you die. *Our Sunday Visitor's Catholic Dictionary* gives two definitions for "saints": "1. Those persons in heaven, whether or not canonized, who lived lives of great charity and heroic virtue. They now live forever with God and share in His glory. 2. Those persons, according to St. Paul, who follow Christ (cf. Col 1:2)." I'm convinced that most of the people who meet those definitions were married.

Nevertheless, it is true that most *canonized* saints were not married. None of the recognized Fathers of the Church — Sts. Ambrose, Augustine, Jerome, Gregory the Great, John Chrysostom, Basil the Great, Gregory of Nazianzen, and Athanasius — were married. Neither were any of the 33 Doctors of the Church — ecclesiastical writers of eminent learning and sanctity who have been given this title because of the great advantage the Church has derived from their work. Still, some of the Church's greatest saints were married — Mary and Joseph, for example, and St. Peter.

The primary purpose of this book is to make it clear that marriage is no obstacle to sanctity. Holiness is possible to married people just as much as it is to popes, pastors, Doctors of the Church, and Religious.

Admittedly, those canonized saints who were married aren't on the Church's role of saints just because they were exemplary spouses. No one has ever been canonized just because he or she was a good wife or husband. Of the married saints profiled in this book, probably St. Monica comes closest to being canonized mainly for the way she fulfilled her vocation as wife and mother. For many — St. Peter, for example—the fact that they were married was incidental to the reasons they are venerated as saints.

In his book *Making Saints*, published in 1990 by Simon and Schuster, Kenneth L. Woodward noted that, of all those who have been beatified or canonized, the one group which is clearly underrepresented is the laity. "Between the year 1000 and the end of 1987, popes held 303 canonizations, including group causes," he wrote. "Of these saints, only 56 were laymen and 20 were laywomen. Moreover, of the 63 lay saints whose state of life is known for certain, more than half never married. And most of these lay saints were martyred, either individually or as members of a group. One might conclude from the lack of married saints that the emotional and sexual satisfactions of a good marriage somehow conflict with the heroic virtue required of a saint."

There is no doubt that the Church historically placed a greater value on virginity than on marriage (even though a validly-contracted marriage is a sacrament). Greatest praise always went to those men and women who renounced "the world" in general or "the flesh" in particular. Even yet today, the saints are placed in categories in apparent descending order of importance — the Blessed Virgin, apostles, martyrs, pastors, Doctors of the Church, virgins, holy men and holy women. There is a category for virgins but not for married men or women.

Some listings of saints seem to go to extreme measures to avoid saying that a particular saint was married. In one book of saints, for example, St. Margaret of Scotland is listed as "widow" even though her husband died only three days before she herself died. One wonders what category she would have been in if she had died four days earlier. Other married saints listed as "widows" rather than "married women" in that book are Frances of Rome, Monica, and Elizabeth of Portugal. Elizabeth Seton, Elizabeth of Hungary, and Bridget of Sweden became Religious after they were widowed, so they are listed under that category. It's interesting, by the way, that all the female married saints in this book were widows except the martyrs Perpetua and Felicity.

Of course, many married saints were also martyrs. This book includes only four of them — St. Thomas More, St. Peter, and Sts. Perpetua and Felicity — because the Church includes them on its liturgical calendar. During the many persecutions the Church has suffered, from the time of the Romans to those during recent centuries, many people who laid down their lives rather than disobey their consciences were married.

I have not tried to identify all the married saints canonized by the Church because I didn't want to write about obscure saints. I limited myself to those memorialized by the Church in its liturgical calendar.

There are four married couples included in this book — Mary and Joseph, Ann and Joachim, Zachary and Elizabeth, and Isidore and Maria. In most cases, however, only one spouse of a married couple has been canonized. Among those currently being considered for canonization by the Vatican are Louis and Zelie Martin, the parents of St. Therese of Lisieux.

In his book *Making Saints*, Kenneth Woodward includes this paragraph about some of the married couples discussed in this book: "There is, it should be noted, a popular impulse among Catholics to impute holiness to the parents of saints, an impulse that goes back to the early Church and its attitude toward figures in the Bible. St. Ann, the otherwise anonymous mother of Mary, is a classic case; so is St. Elizabeth, the mother of John the Baptist. Indeed, if it weren't that their son turned out so well, Mary and Joseph would not be venerated as saints either."

Why aren't there more canonized married saints? Woodward asked that question of Jesuit Father Kurt Peter Gumpel of the Vatican's Congregation of the Causes of Saints. He replied that the lack of married saints was the fault of the Catholic laity. "We all regret that we don't have more candidates who are married. But as you know, causes depend on a reputation for holiness, and as long as lay Catholics do not have a full and total appreciation of marriage as a way to sanctity, then people seeing married people will not even think of them as saints. Unless this happens, there can be no *fama sanctitatis* and thus no causes of married people sent to Rome."

I hope this book might convince more people that they should indeed think about more married people as saints.

However, there is a more practical reason for the lack of more canonized married saints: They have no one to "push" their causes. Religious orders often successfully put forward causes on behalf of their founders or foundresses, as was done for one of our married saints — Elizabeth Ann Seton. The religious orders can usually assign someone to spend a lot of time working on the cause. Dioceses or bishops' conferences can spearhead the causes of deserving individuals. But usually there is no one to do the same thing for married people. The process takes a great deal of time — usually decades or even centuries — and it gets to be expensive. By the time Elizabeth Ann Seton was canonized, the process cost more than $250,000 and before Philadelphia-born Katharine Drexel (not one of the married saints) was declared blessed, at least $333,250 was spent.

With these considerations, it's not surprising that more lay people, and married people in particular, aren't canonized. Those who made it were extraordinary indeed. And that is true of those who appear in this book.

I lead off with my favorite, St. Thomas More. As a man, I can't think of a better role model. This "man for all seasons" was married (twice, after his first wife died); father of four children and foster-father of another; Lord Chancellor of England; one of the greatest authors of the 16th century; and a deeply spiritual man. I have often wondered if he would have been canonized if he hadn't died a martyr. Since he was such an outstanding example of lay spirituality, and since he was so prominent in governmental and literary societies, I think he would have been. But, of course, we'll never know.

If Thomas More is a good role model for married men, many of the female saints in this book could be role models for married women. All 13 of the female saints in this book, by the way, were mothers, but not all 10 of the male saints were fathers. St. Edward the Confessor did not father any children and we're not sure about St. Peter. St. Joseph might or might not have had children by a previous marriage, as I explain in the chapter about Mary and Joseph, but, of course, he was foster-father of Jesus.

Not all of our married saints had large families. St. Louis had the most children — 11. He was followed by St. Margaret of Scotland and St. Bridget with eight, St. Frances of Rome perhaps with six although we know about only three, St. Elizabeth Seton with five, and St. Thomas More with four. Many of them had only one child. With the emphasis the Church historically has placed on large families, it's a bit surprising that more of these saints didn't have more children.

Running down the list of canonized married saints, it's easy to see that those who were "born to the purple" had more of a chance than peasants. Perhaps Isidore and Maria are the exception that proves the rule. Four kings are included — Louis, Stephen, Henry and Edward — as well as three queens — Elizabeth of Hungary, Elizabeth of Portugal and Margaret of Scotland. Undoubtedly their prominence had a lot to do with the fact that they were canonized, but perhaps the contrast between their holiness and that of many other members of royalty also contributed. That contrast was particularly evident in the case of St. Bridget of Sweden.

The profiles that follow are not intended to be complete biographies. They are meant to explain why the Church considers these men and women holy enough to be included in its roster of saints, as much about their married lives as we know, and perhaps what modern married men and women can learn from them. Some chapters are shorter than others simply because we know less about those particular saints. Above all, I hope to show that the term "married saint" is not an oxymoron. It is not a contradiction of terms.

I guess we married people can take pride that at least some of our peers made it.

ST. THOMAS MORE

Many people know Thomas More mainly because of his dispute with King Henry VIII of England, which resulted in his execution. But Thomas More was much more than that. That's why he was called "A Man for All Seasons" by Robert Bolt in the play by that name. Actually, it was Desiderius Erasmus, More's friend, who first used that phrase to describe More.

Thomas More is a man that most of us can emulate, especially married men and women. It's true that he might not have been canonized had he not been martyred but, if not, he should have been. He is possibly the best example of a man who could be eminently successful in secular life while still maintaining the religious practices that can make anyone a saint. He was also a husband and a father who knew what it was like to live in the bedlam of hectic family life.

More is known in literary circles as one of the best authors of the Renaissance. He was widely known as both a poet and an author. A chronology of his published works lists 30 writings, and *The Complete Works of Thomas More*, published by Yale University Press, consists of 15 large volumes. The most famous of his works was *Utopia*, the literary masterpiece he wrote when he was 39 years old. This book opened the door to friendship with other literary figures of his time, although he had been great friends with Erasmus since he first met him when he was only 22. More hosted mainly literary figures and educators at his home; one of the things he was known for was his talents as a host.

Thomas More was born on February 7, 1477 in London, to John and Agnes More. His mother died when he was a child and was not an influence on him. His father, though, John More, very definitely was. (His father, by the way, married four times in his 79 years.) Like Thomas, John More was a lawyer and he attended very closely to Thomas's personal and professional development. Left to his own preferences, Thomas would not have become a lawyer since his preferences in school were for theology and the other liberal arts — literature, history, and philosophy. Like many scholars of his time, he became fluent in both Latin and Greek. In fact, he wrote *Utopia* in Latin for the intelligentsia of Europe. It was translated into English after his death.

Thomas studied at Oxford from age 14 to 16, was a pre-law student in London from 16 to 18, a law student at Lincoln's Inn in London from 18 to 23, and was called to the bar at age 23.

During this time, and after, Thomas was questioning his vocation in life. For the next four years, he lived in the London Charterhouse, a Carthusian monastery, where he participated in the monks' life of prayer and learned their ways of austere living. He worked at developing his prayer life and achieving self-mastery, beginning the spiritual practices that he would maintain the rest of his life. While in his early 20's he began to wear a hair shirt — a shirt with hair against the skin. He limited the number of hours he slept, and fasted regularly.

His biographers tell us that, until his imprisonment, he rose each morning at 2 o'clock, a practice he started while living with the Carthusians. Of course, it's true that people in Tudor times in England rose earlier, and retired earlier, making full use of daylight. More's 2 a.m. was perhaps equivalent to 4 a.m. in our society. He started each day with prayer, including the Divine Office, followed by study and attendance at Mass.

In struggling with his vocation, More finally discerned that his calling was definitely to married life. According to Erasmus, More decided that his calling was to become "a chaste husband rather than a licentious priest." More himself wrote that, during his adolescence, his struggle with his sexuality brought him almost to the "very gates of hell."

In one of his writings when he was 41, he wrote about his father's parental wisdom when More, then 16, had become infatuated with a 14-year-old girl. "On his account," More wrote, "a chaperon was imposed upon us, and a door strong enough to thwart our very destiny kept apart a pair whom the stars wished to bring together."

So More discerned that his calling from God was to married life. At age 28 he married Jane Colt. The children came quickly — four children in five-and-a-half years — three girls and a boy. Meanwhile, Thomas's law practice was growing quickly and he was beginning to make a name for himself with his writings. Life was very good for Thomas More.

And then tragedy struck. Jane More became ill and died, quite unexpectedly. Apart from his grief, Thomas had the pressing difficulty of caring for four young children. Against the advice of his friends and common custom, he remarried within 30 days of Jane's death. Within his wide circle of friends he knew many available women, and he chose Alice Middleton, a woman seven years older than he. He was 33, she 40. There is evidence that the marriage was not always a happy one, but, as More wrote to a friend, "I do not think it possible to live, even with the best of wives, without some discomfort. However, generally we make our wives worse by our own faults."

As a parent, Thomas More was exceptional

for a man of the 16th century. He insisted that his daughters receive as excellent an education as his son. This is another important part of More as "a man for all seasons." In the history of education, Thomas More holds an important place — a distinction that was recognized even in his own day. The education he planned and supervised for his children was, in fact, so successful that the school in his home became famous throughout Europe. Some of his closest friends were the most noted educators of Christendom, classical scholars who wrote a great deal about education.

In a letter to William Gonell, his children's teacher, More explained his philosophy of education. Regardless of the subject, he wrote, Gonell should "esteem most whatever may teach them piety towards God, charity to all, and modesty and Christian humility in themselves. The whole fruit of their endeavors should consist in the testimony of God and good conscience. Thus they will be inwardly calm and at peace and neither stirred by the praise of flatterers nor stung by the follies of unlearned mockers of learning."

More was host to many men of learning. Before the evening was over, though, he would lead all those present — his family and guests — in Night Prayer.

In addition to his four natural children, Thomas and Alice also had an adopted daughter and a ward for whom they cared.

Thomas lived a life of intense study, particularly during his 20's and 30's. His friend Erasmus wrote of him, "His early years were exercised principally in poetry; after that came a long struggle to acquire a more supple style in prose by practicing his pen in every sort of writing." More worked on developing his powers of expression. He set up friendly contests with some of the greatest rhetoricians of his time.

He also entered politics, being elected a member of Parliament at age 27 by the London merchants he worked for as a lawyer. His reputation as a lawyer grew, particularly his reputation for honesty and integrity. He was undersheriff of London from age 33 to 41, a position that involved advising the sheriff and mayor on legal issues. Our equivalent would be the office of city attorney, except that More's position also involved the responsibility of presiding as judge in the sheriff's court. More carried out his work as judge every Thursday morning.

By the time More reached his 40's, he had become the most successful lawyer in England. Because of his reputation for integrity and prudent judgment, both as a lawyer and as a judge, More's law practice grew enormously and he became quite wealthy. His son-in-law, William Roper, says that he made 400 pounds a year — a substantial sum considering that the ordinary person lived on 10 pounds a year. More used his money for social, educational, and spiritual projects.

He also bought a 34-acre estate at Chelsea, two miles from London on the Thames River, when he was 47. By this time his children started to have their own children — 11 grandchildren were born before More was imprisoned — and he wanted them all to be together. Here at Chelsea, King Henry would occasionally visit and walk with More through extensive gardens and orchards.

The home at Chelsea has been called spacious rather than magnificent. It was large enough to accommodate the families of his four children as well as friends who would visit. One biographer says that More may have been supporting as many as 40 people — his family, in-laws, grandchildren, stepchildren, foster children, tutors, servants and secretaries. His son-in-law, Giles Heron, managed the estate for him. More traveled to his offices in London by barge on the Thames.

However, there is such a thing as too much togetherness, so Thomas also had constructed a building at the corner of his property, fairly distant from his busy home, that housed his private chapel, library and gallery. There he retired to study, pray and write — sometimes for the whole day.

More's career continued to spiral upward. At age 46 he was elected Speaker of the House of Commons, where he championed free speech centuries before it became a political issue. When he was 52 King Henry appointed him Lord Chancellor of England, the highest appointive office in England. The greatest responsibility of the Lord Chancellor was to serve as the chief justice of England. Legal historian John Guy tells us that, in this office, More handled an average of 912 cases per year, compared to 535 cases handled by Wolsey when he was chancellor. Guy reviewed the archival records of the 2,356 suits which came before the chancery during More's 31 months in office. He said that More "cultivated a distinctive policy of self-involvement, scrupulousness, and discretion. In the last resort, his great contribution was exactly this: to rejuvenate the ancient theory that judges had a personal duty in conscience to see right done by all whose business was entertained in the courts they directed."

Then More opposed King Henry VIII's divorce and remarriage, was forced to resign, was later imprisoned, refused to recant, and was finally executed on July 6, 1535 when he was 58 years old.

What was Thomas More's personality like? One telling thing is that he was sometimes called in his own day "merry More." He seemed always to be joyful, in fact full of wit. More himself saw this as one of his faults. He realized that a constant joker can endear but can also irritate. Sometimes his wit irritated. For example, he had a great friendship with Francis Cranevelt and his wife

Elizabeth, but he apparently went too far in his joking with Francis. At the end of one letter, he signed off with, "Farewell to your wife — mine by day, yours by night." And later he wrote, just as playfully, "As for my mistress your wife, or rather your mistress my wife, since I betrothed myself to her there long since...." This jesting apparently got under Francis' skin because More repented in a subsequent letter.

Edward Hall, a contemporary historian, said of More: "Undoubtedly he had, besides his learning, a great wit, but it was so mingled with taunting and mocking that it seemed to them that best knew him, that he thought it nothing to be well spoken unless he had ministered some mock in the communication."

He couldn't keep from jesting even as he was being led to his execution. That same Edward Hall mentioned five jests More made as he was being prepared for execution. I'll mention two: As he went up the steps he asked for help (his health had deteriorated while he was in prison) but said, "When I come down again, let me shift for myself as well as I can." As he lay his neck on the block to have it cut off, he signaled the executioner to wait. The beard he had grown while in prison was lying on the block and he asked if he could remove it. At least that had committed no treason, he said.

Erasmus said of More that he was "born and

made for friendship." He simply enjoyed people and usually tried to be friendly. It is said that he habitually turned aside offensive comments with a lighthearted remark or artfully but forcefully changed the topic of conversation. Even in court, when he recognized that he was on the winning side, he used his humor and wit to keep from seeming too harsh.

His spirituality was an important part of his personality. I've already mentioned his prayer life and his penances. He was also a good parishioner of the church that he supported in the village of Chelsea, singing in the choir on Sundays and serving at Mass on weekdays even while he was chancellor of England. He personally visited the poor of the parish and eventually rented a building to care for poor villagers, providing for them at his expense and entrusting their care to his own children.

More loved the psalms. Some of them were part of his daily prayers, particularly the seven penitential psalms. He made notations in his Psalter which, by the way, was in Latin. Of course, that posed no problem for More. For Night Prayer with his family he chose Psalms 51, 25, 67 and 130, the *De Profundis*. Toward the end of his life he wrote an extended commentary on Psalm 91, and while in prison he collected verses from 31 psalms to form one powerful prayer he could pray from his prison cell. His last prayer on earth was Psalm 51, the *Miserere*.

Many of More's writings were on religious subjects, beginning with his first book, published when he was 27. It was *The Life of John Picus*, an outstanding Italian layman and intellectual whom More saw as a model for his own life. He didn't write this book but translated it from Latin into English. This book included two poems, "The Twelve Rules of Spiritual Battle" and "The Twelve Weapons of Spiritual Battle."

More's last book dealt with, as he put it, "the story of that time when the apostles were sleeping as the Son of Man was being betrayed." The apostles represented Church leaders who fell asleep at their posts, a veiled criticism of the Church leaders of his day who went along with King Henry VIII.

One of More's works was *The Four Last Things (Quattuor Novissima)*, which he wrote when he was 45. This was really written for his children and he didn't expect it to be published. It was a meditation on death, judgment, heaven and hell. The topic reflects the fact that More often meditated on the meaning of the passion and death of Christ — that Christ died for each of us. This was very real to him. One of his last works was *A Treatise Upon the Passion*.

Another thing that was very real to him was the Scripture quotation: *What does it profit a man if he gain the whole world but suffer the loss of his soul?* He wrote that even the greatest of earthly pleasures is "little, simple, short, and suddenly past." Why, he asked, would any sane person buy a momentary pleasure for an eternity of pain? Furthermore, he said, if we would compare all the pleasures of this world, we would discover that the greatest by far is a clear conscience.

It was entirely because his conscience would not allow him to condone Henry's actions that he was in prison and condemned to death. Many times his family tried to persuade him to sign the oath that would free him from prison. They criticized him for what they called his "scruple of conscience." According to his son-in-law, William Roper, when his wife Alice called him a fool for remaining in a filthy prison with rats and mice when he could be free, Thomas asked her, "How long, my Alice, shall I be able to enjoy this life?"

"A full 20 years, if God so wills," Alice replied.

Thomas said: "Do you wish me, then, to exchange eternity for 20 years? Here, good wife, you do not bargain very skillfully."

No one begged Thomas to sign the oath more than did his daughter Margaret, or Meg. He called her "mistress Eve, come to tempt her father again." He also told her that he considered his imprisonment as a sign of God's special love for him because it gave him the opportunity to prepare for his death.

Thomas wrote many letters to his daughter

Margaret from prison, trying to make her understand his position. The letters show that he was completely resigned to follow God's will, whatever that might be. Here is an extensive quotation from one of those letters:

"Although I know well, Margaret, that because of my past wickedness I deserve to be abandoned by God, I cannot but trust in His merciful goodness. His grace has strengthened me until now and made me content to lose goods, land, and life as well, rather than to swear against my conscience. God's grace has given the king a gracious frame of mind toward me, so that as yet he has taken from me nothing but my liberty. In doing this His Majesty has done me such good with respect to spiritual profit that I trust that among all the great benefits he has heaped so abundantly upon me I count my imprisonment the very greatest. I cannot, therefore, mistrust the grace of God. Either He shall keep the king in that gracious frame of mind to continue to do me no harm, or else, if it be His pleasure that for my other sins I suffer in this case as I shall not deserve, then His grace shall give me the strength to bear it patiently, and perhaps even gladly.

"By the merits of His bitter passion joined to mine and far surpassing in merit for me all that I can suffer myself, His bounteous goodness shall release me from the pains of purgatory and shall increase my reward in heaven besides.

"I will not mistrust Him, Meg, though I shall feel myself weakening and on the verge of being overcome with fear. I shall remember how St. Peter at a blast of wind began to sink because of his lack of faith, and I shall do as he did: call upon Christ and pray to Him for help. And then I trust He shall place His holy hand on me and in the stormy seas hold me up from drowning.

"And if He permits me to play St. Peter further and to fall to the ground and to swear and forswear, may God our Lord in His tender mercy keep me from this, and let me lose if it so happen, and never win thereby! Still, if this should happen, afterward I trust that in His goodness He will look on me with pity as He did upon St. Peter, and make me stand up again and confess the trust of my conscience afresh and endure here the shame and harm of my own fault.

"And finally, Margaret, I know this well: that without my fault He will not let me be lost. I shall, therefore, with good hope commit myself wholly to Him. And if He permits me to perish for my faults, then I shall serve as praise for His justice. But in good faith, Meg, I trust that His tender pity shall keep my poor soul safe and make me commend His mercy.

"And, therefore, my own good daughter, do not let your mind be troubled over anything that shall happen to me in this world. Nothing can come but what God wills. And I am very sure that whatever that be, however bad it may seem, it shall indeed be the best."

So, with that final lesson to his daughter, Thomas More went to his death rather than violate his conscience. That is why he was canonized in 1935, four centuries after his death. But his virtues were recognized widely well before that and he was admired before the dispute with Henry VIII ever arose. Two centuries after his death Jonathan Swift called him "a person of the greatest virtue this kingdom ever produced," and poet John Donne described him as a "man of the most tender and delicate conscience that the world saw since Augustine."

A man who demonstrated that one can live a holy life in a secular world, and who clearly saw his vocation as a husband and a father, St. Thomas More is a perfect role model for each of us.

He was canonized in 1935. His feast day is celebrated on June 22.

ST. ELIZABETH ANN SETON

Perhaps we can take some pride in the fact that the first North American-born citizen to be canonized was a wife and a mother. She was also the foundress of the parochial school system and the first Religious Order in the United States. Her spirituality was extraordinary and her trial—she called them "holocausts"—were severe, but she is certainly a saint that any mother can approach knowing that she has a sympathetic ear.

The first half of her life gave no indication that Elizabeth would end up doing the things that she did. She was then a Protestant, born August 28, 1774 (two years before the Declaration of Independence and the start of the Revolutionary War) into the wealthy and distinguished New York Bayley family. However, by the time she was 30 she was a widow with five children, living in poverty. When she converted to Catholicism she was ostracized from New York society and had to flee to Baltimore to support her family.

Eventually, Elizabeth Ann Seton was known

as Mother Seton. She founded an Order of Sisters and based its rule on that of a French Order, the Daughters of Charity of St. Vincent de Paul. Today the Daughters of Charity serve and staff hospitals, colleges, high schools and elementary schools, homes for unwed mothers, clinics, services for the elderly, and numerous other charities. The Daughters of Charity, along with the Archdiocese of Baltimore, spearheaded efforts for her canonization and it is undoubtedly true that she wouldn't have been canonized solely because of her role as a wife and mother. Just as Thomas More probably wouldn't have been canonized if he hadn't been martyred, but should have been, so it is with Elizabeth Seton: Her holiness was so pronounced as she fulfilled her roles as wife and mother that she could have been canonized for that reason alone.

Elizabeth's mother was Catherine Charlton, the daughter of the Episcopalian Rector of St. Andrew's Church, Staten Island. She died when Elizabeth was only three years old. Her father was Dr. Richard Bayley, a renowned physician as well as professor of anatomy at King's College in New York, an institution that later developed into Columbia University. Elizabeth was reared by her father as a staunch Episcopalian. As such, she learned the value of prayer, Scripture, and a nightly examination of conscience. Although Dr. Bayley seldom went to church, he was known as a great humanitarian and he taught his daughter to love and serve others.

Elizabeth's education was similar to that of other high society girls in New York during the 18th century. She learned music, French, literature, sewing, dancing, and the skills necessary for a housewife. She took a particular interest in history and religious literature, taking full advantage of her father's extensive library. She was greatly influenced by Thomas à Kempis' book *The Imitation of Christ* and, of course, the Bible. She began practices that were more Catholic than Episcopalian — wearing a crucifix, bowing her head at the name of Jesus, praying to her guardian angel.

By her late teens, Elizabeth Bayley was the belle of New York, widely courted by the city's gentlemen. When she was 19, she chose William Magee Seton for her husband, a wealthy merchant six years older than she. He was a well-traveled young man, having done business in France and Spain as well as in Italy, where he had been apprenticed to the Filicchi family, a family of bankers and shipbuilders.

Their wedding on January 25, 1794 was one of New York's principal social events of the winter. Then, for the next 11 years, Elizabeth and William Seton were a model of the perfect young wealthy American family of that era. There can be no doubt of her love for him. Her entries in her diaries always refer to him as "my William." Their five children, three girls and two boys, were born within eight years. She became very close to William's sisters Rebecca, Harriet and Cecilia, all of whom remained loyal to her in years to come.

One note of sadness during that time was the death of Elizabeth's father. He contracted yellow fever while attending to some Irish immigrants with that disease. Elizabeth, who was about to have her fifth child, rushed to his bedside. Repeatedly calling, "My Christ Jesus, have mercy on me," he died in Elizabeth's arms.

During all this period, Elizabeth's diary shows a deepening of her spirituality, a spirituality she tried to impart to her children — Anna Maria (later called Annina), William, Richard, Catherine (sometimes called Josephine or Kit) and Rebecca. She faithfully attended services at Trinity Episcopal Church, where she came under the influence of Rev. Henry Hobart. Unfortunately, he was bitterly anti-Catholic.

This happy family life took an abrupt change in 1803, when Elizabeth was 29. Her husband's health and business both began to fail. William Seton, suffering from blood in his lungs and dysentery, made the decision to sail to Italy to visit the Filicchis, somehow thinking that his health would improve in Italy. Elizabeth knew that she had to accompany William because someone had to care for him. By this time their wealth had dwindled to such an extent that they could take only one child with them, their oldest daughter Anna Maria. The other four children were left with friends.

They sailed on a ship called *The Shepherd-ess* under the command of a Captain O'Brien and his wife. They were the only passengers. The passage was not a pleasant one. It took 56 days to get to Italy, with William's health continuing to deteriorate and with Anna Maria contracting whooping cough. Elizabeth, of course, had to nurse them both.

Then further problems rose. When they arrived at Italy, jubilant at the thought of getting off the ship, they learned that they could not enter Italy immediately. There had been another attack of yellow fever in New York and *The Shepherdess* didn't have a bill of health to show that its passengers were free of the disease. So the Setons were quarantined in a "pesthouse" on the shore, called a Lazaretto. William had to be carried there and little Anna Maria trembled with fright. A guard was posted to keep the family in the Lazaretto. It was a prison.

Here is a passage from Elizabeth's diary while in the Lazaretto: "Here my husband, who left all to seek a milder climate, is confined in this high place and within these damp walls, exposed to the cold and to the dreary winds that penetrate to the very bones; without fire except the charcoal which oppresses his breast so as nearly to convulse him; no little syrups, nor soother of his cough; bark, warm milk, and opium pills (which he takes quietly as a duty, without seeming to hope) is all I can offer him from day to day. When nature fails, and I can no longer look up with cheerfulness, I hide my face in my hands on the chair by his bedside, and he thinks I am praying; and pray I do, for prayer is all my comfort; without it I should be of little service to him. Night and day he calls me his life, his soul, his dearest of women, his all."

These were the conditions the little family lived in from November 19 to December 19, 1803. William's health continued to decline. On December 19, he was carried out of the pesthouse and taken by coach to a house in Pisa. It had been 96 days since they left their home in New York.

William lived only eight more days. Elizabeth spent the last night kneeling by his side reading prayers. William told her to tell his friends that he died happy, satisfied with the Divine Will. With the name of Jesus on his lips, he died. The scene was almost identical to that of the death of Elizabeth's father.

Elizabeth was now a widow. She moved into the home of the Filicchis in Italy until she could return to New York. The Filicchi brothers, Filippo and Antonio, were devout Catholics as well as successful businessmen. Filippo had married an American woman and was a friend of Washington, Jefferson, Madison, John Adams, and John Carroll, the first Catholic bishop of Baltimore. Antonio had married an Italian woman, Amabilia, and these two were to become Elizabeth's closest friends and supporters.

It wasn't long before the most important topic for discussion in the Filicchi household was religion. Elizabeth felt spiritually at home with this family that began each day with Mass and where devotion to the Blessed Mother included the daily saying of the rosary. Elizabeth was particularly excited by three basic points of Catholicism: belief in the real presence of Jesus in the Blessed Sacrament, devotion to Mary the Mother of God, and conviction that the Catholic Church could be traced back to Christ and his apostles.

Elizabeth and Anna Maria tried to return to New York in February, again aboard *The Shepherdess*. However, a severe storm drove the ship back. Furthermore, Anna Maria came down with a high fever and a doctor told Elizabeth that Anna Maria could not survive the journey. The Setons returned to the Filicchi mansion. Then Elizabeth herself caught Anna Maria's illness and it seemed for a while that she would not recover. But she did eventually and she and Anna Maria were ready again to sail back to New York to rejoin Elizabeth's other four children.

By this time, though, *The Shepherdess* had already sailed. The new ship was called *The Flamingo*. Now a new problem rose: Elizabeth and Anna Maria were to be the only passengers and no one knew much about the captain, whose name was Blagg. So Antonio and Amabilia decided that Antonio should accompany them to New York. He had business to attend to there anyway.

There was another two-month journey on the Atlantic Ocean before Elizabeth was reunited with her other four children. It was a trip during which she learned much more about the Catholic faith from Antonio, who had prepared a syllabus of Catholic teachings for her.

Shortly after her return to New York, Elizabeth was again at the bedside while a dear one died. This time it was her sister-in-law Rebecca, the confidante of all her diary entries from the time of her departure to Italy until her return. After Rebecca's death, there is a difference in Elizabeth's diary entries. One biographer wrote that "the verve of her writings up to this moment will be diminished" because "Rebecca was the only one to whom one should and could tell *all*."

The next few years were very hard for Elizabeth. Some of her problems were financial. She knew, but William did not when he died, that the family fortune was gone. William had left a will disposing of many possessions that he no longer owned and Elizabeth had obeyed William's doctors who thought it best that he not know that he had lost his wealth. Now Elizabeth had to support herself and her five children.

At the same time, she struggled with her decision about whether to remain an Episcopalian or to become a Catholic. She was torn between following her beliefs and the admonitions of her friends that she not abandon the faith of her family. She finally made up her mind to become a Catholic and was formally received into the Catholic Church on March 14, 1805. She was 30 years old.

It's hard today to imagine what this decision did to Elizabeth in the eyes of New York society. She was immediately forsaken by most of her family and friends, with the notable exceptions of her two surviving sisters-in-law Cecilia and Harriet Seton, and Julia Scott of Philadelphia. Elizabeth's children, on the other hand, were very happy because they were well aware that making this hard decision had damaged her health. On the day of her First Communion, Elizabeth wrote to Amabilia Filicchi, "My health is pitiful."

But with five children to support, she had to find a job. She had humbly accepted financial help from the Filicchis but knew that her family was her responsibility. First she was invited by an Englishman named White to help him open a school in New York. The school lasted only three months before it had to be closed.

Then an incident happened that convinced Elizabeth that she had to get out of New York. Cecilia Seton, her sister-in-law, became seriously sick and Elizabeth went to care for her. During her convalescence, Cecilia confided that she wanted to become a Catholic like Elizabeth. When she told her family, they were outraged and blamed Elizabeth. They locked Cecilia in her room and demanded that she break off all relations with the "corrupter of her mind." They even threatened to deport her to the West Indies. But Cecilia finally prevailed and became a Catholic.

Now Elizabeth was determined to get out of New York. The chance finally came when Father William Du Bourg, the president of St. Mary's Seminary in Baltimore, invited her to open a school for girls in Baltimore. The school opened in June of 1808. It was the first parochial school in the United States. Elizabeth and her children lived in a house on Paca Street with Father Du Bourg's mother and sister.

That summer a priest at St. Mary's Seminary in Baltimore, who had been acting as chaplain for Elizabeth's school, met a girl in Philadelphia, Cecilia O'Conway, who expressed interest in becoming a nun. He told her about Elizabeth Seton and the school in Baltimore and soon Cecilia came to Baltimore. Shortly afterward, Samuel Sutherland Cooper, a wealthy man who decided to become a priest, donated some of his property in Emmitsburg, 50 miles west of Baltimore, to Elizabeth. Almost without her planning, the nucleus of a religious community was developing.

Soon there were five women aspiring to become nuns. In the spring of 1809, after conferences with Bishop John Carroll, they formally formed a religious community, calling themselves the Sisters of St. Joseph. Elizabeth was elected their superior and from then on was known as Mother Seton.

The community moved to the property in Emmitsburg where, despite extreme hardships for a number of years, the Order continued to expand. It also, upon the advice of Bishop Carroll, eventually adopted the rule of an existing community. The Sisters chose the Daughters of Charity of St. Vincent de Paul and the Order was known from then on as the Daughters of Charity of St. Joseph.

Two of the women who followed Mother Seton were her two sisters-in-law, Cecilia and Harriet. Both were in frail health, though, and both ended up dying in Elizabeth's arms, just as their sister Rebecca and their brother William had done.

Mother Seton continued to lead her community for another 12 years. It spread rapidly. Before her death there were 20 Daughters of Charity communities spread across the United States. The Sisters established orphanages and hospitals, but were most renowned for their commitment to the spread of the parochial school system.

As for Mother Seton, she somehow found time to work personally with the poor and the sick, to compose music, write hymns and prepare spiritual discourses, especially for her Sisters. These discourses usually had as their theme abandonment to the will of God. In one of her discourses, she said, "The first end I propose in our daily work is to do the will of God; secondly, to do it in the manner he wills it; and thirdly, to do it because it is his will."

Mother Seton also continued to care for her children. This was something she felt strongly about. The original French rule of the Daughters of Charity specified that widows with children seeking to enter the Order must see that the children are provided for and cared for by others. Mother Seton absolutely refused. She wrote to one friend, "By the law of the Church I so much love, I could never take an obligation which interfered with my duties to my children, except I had an independent guardian and provision for them, which the whole world could not supply, to my judgment of a mother's duty."

And to another she wrote, "My dear children have the first right which must ever remain inviolable. That is why I have made a solemn engagement before our good archbishop, as well as my own conscience, to prefer before all things the advantage of my children, if it happened that I had to choose between what I owe to them and other duties to which I was pledged."

Her oldest child, Anna Maria, became a postulant in the Emmitsburg community. But her health was never very good, and she died on March 12, 1812, with Elizabeth and Anna Maria's sisters, Catherine and Rebecca, at her bedside. Elizabeth had previously helped her father, her husband, and three sisters-in-law enter eternity. This time it was one of her children.

And it was not the last. Little Rebecca, the

youngest child, fell on the ice while ice skating one winter day. She cracked her spine and was unable to walk again. She was put under the care of the best surgeons in the United States at that time, but her health continued to decline. She died in 1815 when she was only 14. Accounts of her death are quite inspirational.

Catherine, or Kit, was the second of Eliza beth's two daughters. After her mother's death, Catherine and her brother William took a trip to Europe. But then she, too, became a nun — not, however, in her mother's community. She eventually became Mother Catherine Seton of the Sisters of Mercy, working with the poor and with prisoners in New York. She died at age 91.

The two Seton boys were sent to Georgetown College, with their tuition and expenses paid for by Antonio Filicchi. The younger boy, Richard, left Georgetown to try to learn banking from the Filicchis. That didn't work out and very little is known about Richard after that. One biographer says that Mother Seton suffered "the heartache of a wayward son." However, we know that he died at age 26 from a disease he contracted while nursing a sick priest.

Elizabeth's oldest son, William, also tried his hand at banking with the Filicchis for two years after he left Georgetown. But banking was not for him. He wanted to be a sailor and became a midshipman in the U.S. Navy. His mother continued to send letters to him, constantly encouraging him in his faith. One biographer wrote: "In his wanderings around the world, on his various boats, William was followed by a series of letters from his mother into which was poured such a torrent of tenderness as to make Monica's tears over Augustine seem almost mild in comparison. If there have been any more rapturous love-letters from a mother to a son ever penned, I certainly have never come across them."

But the letters reached him only sporadically. Mother and son did not see each other during the last four years of Mother Seton's life. Finally, William had a chance to visit Emmitsburg and biographers describe an emotional scene of his running to the convent only to learn that she had died six months before. William went to the small cemetery where he found the graves of his mother, two sisters and two aunts.

William was the only one of Elizabeth's children to marry. One of his children became an archbishop.

Mother Elizabeth Ann Seton was only 46 when she died on January 4, 1821, with her whole community of Sisters around her. Her last word was "Jesus." She was canonized September 24, 1975. Her feast day is celebrated on January 4.

ST. MONICA

I s there anyone who doesn't know St. Monica? She is the patron saint of all mothers as well as of married women, housewives, alcoholics, and those who are victims of infidelity.

St. Monica is known today because she had a famous son. Indeed, the only things we know about Monica came from the writings of her son, St. Augustine, especially his *Confessions*. St. Augustine is not only one of the 33 Doctors of the Church but also one of the four Fathers of the Western Church. (The others are Sts. Ambrose, Jerome and Gregory the Great.) Even today more of the writings of St. Augustine are included in the Office of Readings, which is part of the Liturgy of the Hours, than those of any other writer, and he is quoted in the *Catechism of the Catholic Church* more often than any other ecclesiastical writer. But if it had not been for the prayers and perseverance of St. Monica, the Church would not have had the benefit of Augustine's wisdom.

Considering the trials Monica faced, she

could easily have become an unhappy wife, a bitter daughter-in-law and a despairing mother. She is a saint because she did not give in to any of those temptations.

Monica was born around the year 332 in Tagaste, North Africa, in what today is Algeria. Her parents were wealthy Christians who employed servants. One of those servants was an elderly woman who was put in charge of Monica and her sisters. Monica told Augustine, who reported it in his *Confessions*, that she owed the discipline she learned, not to her mother, but to this elderly maidservant who "restrained them earnestly, when necessary, with a holy severity, and taught them with a grave discretion."

One of the things this maid-servant insisted on was that the girls not drink anything between meals, even water. Her reasoning was: "You drink water now because you don't have wine in your power; but when you come to be married and are made mistresses of cellars and cupboards, you will scorn water but the custom of drinking will continue."

This discipline backfired for Monica though. She was frequently sent by her parents to the wine cellar to get wine for dinner and she soon fell in the habit of taking secret sips. At first she sipped some from the tips of her fingers but, as she acquired a taste for the wine, she soon was drinking full cups. However, a young servant with whom she went to the cellar started taunting her, calling her a wine-bibber. Monica, Augustine wrote, "stung to the quick, saw the foulness of her fault, and instantly condemned and forsook it." It was this episode that made her a patron saint of alcoholics.

When Monica reached marriageable age, her parents found a husband for her, as was the custom at the time. Augustine does not tell us why Monica's parents chose a pagan rather than a Christian, but they did. They chose Patricius, a man known to have a violent temper. Furthermore, he was unfaithful to her, which is why she is the patron saint of victims of infidelity. Augustine wrote: "She so endured the wronging of her bed as never to have any quarrel with her husband thereon. For she looked for Thy mercy upon him, that believing in Thee, he might be made chaste."

Monica put up with much more from her husband than most modern women ever would have, and she did it with kindness and gentleness. Augustine wrote: "In a word, while many matrons, who had milder husbands, yet bore even in their faces marks of shame, would in familiar talk blame their husbands' lives, she would blame their tongues, giving them, as in jest, earnest advice: 'That from the time they heard the marriage writings read to them, they should account them as indentures, whereby they were made servants; and so, remembering their condition, ought not to set themselves up against their lords.'"

The Church does not teach that a wife must make herself a servant to her husband and, in his teaching while an archbishop, Augustine always impressed on men the respect, affection and consideration they owed their wives. It was the society in which they lived that treated women as subject to their husbands, and, as Augustine's words indicate, wife beating was common. Monica obviously felt herself bound to serve Patricius and made sure she did so cheerfully despite the things Patricius did.

Apparently it was prudent of her to do so, if she had to live with Patricius. Augustine wrote: "And when other women, knowing what a choleric husband she endured, marveled that it had never been heard, nor by any token perceived, that Patricius had beaten his wife, or that there had been any domestic difference between them, even for one day, and confidentially asking the reason, she taught them her practice above mentioned. Those wives who observed it found the good, and returned thanks; those who observed it not, found no relief, and suffered."

Monica also had to put up with a difficult mother-in-law who lived with her and Patricius. Augustine says that Monica's mother-in-law was "at first by whisperings of evil servants incensed against her." But because of Monica's "persevering endurance and meekness," her mother-in-law was won over. She even had her son Patricius whip the servants who spoke ill of Monica and "she promised the like reward to any who, to please her, should speak ill of her daughter-in-law to her." The result was that "they lived together with a remarkable sweetness of mutual kindness."

Meanwhile, Patricius continued to criticize Monica's Christian faith. Slowly but surely, though, he was won over through Monica's prayers and example. A year before his death, which happened when Augustine was 17, Patricius too became a Christian.

Monica and Patricius had three children: Augustine, Navigius and Perpetua. Apparently Navigius was always an exemplary son and Perpetua became a religious and an abbess. It was only Augustine who caused Monica so much pain.

He was the more brilliant of the two sons. When he was barely 12 years old, he was sent to a grammar school at Madaura, where he received a rigorous education. He was forced to learn and to apply himself, and the system worked very well. Augustine was a student for the rest of his life.

When he returned to Tagaste at 16, though, he soon fell into loose company, as can easily happen to boys in their middle teens. Monica pleaded with him to govern his passions but, as he said, her words "seemed to me but the admonitions of a woman, which I was ashamed to obey."

After Patricius died, a wealthy man paid Augustine's expenses to study in Carthage, one of the great centers of learning in the fourth century. He quickly advanced to the top of his class in the school of rhetoric. However, he also began a relationship with a woman whom he was to keep by his side for more than 13 years. Before he was 20 he was the father of a son, whom he named Adeodatus, which meant Given by God.

Not only was he living an immoral life, but he also came under the influence of the Manichaeans. Manichaeism was a heresy based on the assumption that two supreme principles (good and evil) are operative in creation and life, and that the supreme objective of human endeavor is liberation from evil (matter). The heresy denied the humanity of Christ, the sacramental system of the Church, and the authority of the Church.

All this greatly upset Monica. For a while, she refused to let him eat or sleep in her house when he was in Tagaste. One day, while she was weeping about her problems, she had a vision. A figure appeared and asked her why she was crying. When she replied that she was weeping about her son, the figure told her to dry her tears because "your son is with you." Later, she told Augustine about her vision. He said that there would be no problems between the two if Monica would give up her faith. Monica quickly replied, "He did not say I was with you; he said that you were with me."

Shortly after that, Monica took her problems to a bishop, who advised her to be patient. He assured her that "it is not possible that the son of so many tears should perish," and that Augustine would return to the faith. From then on, Monica stayed as close as possible to Augustine, praying and fasting for his conversion. She got much closer than Augustine wanted.

When he was 29, Augustine decided to go to Rome to teach rhetoric there. Monica opposed the move, but Augustine went anyway, along with his mistress and son. He opened a school in Rome, but it was unsuccessful financially. He then moved on to Milan, where a position was open for a teacher of rhetoric. Augustine applied for it and received the appointment.

Monica followed Augustine to Milan, along with her other son Navigius. There both Monica and Augustine came under the influence of St. Ambrose, Milan's powerful and learned bishop. Monica took her problems to him while quickly becoming a leader of the devout women in the city.

Coming from North Africa, Monica found some of the religious practices of Milan quite different from what she was accustomed to. She asked Ambrose which customs she should follow, mentioning specifically her practice of fasting on Saturdays, something that was not done in Milan but was done at that time in both Tagaste and in Rome.

Ambrose replied, "When I am here, I do not fast on Saturday, but I fast when I am in Rome; do the same and always follow the custom and discipline of the Church as it is observed in the particular locality in which you find yourself." This has been boiled down to the classic quotation, "When in Rome, do as the Romans do."

Augustine came under Ambrose's influence mainly as a result of Ambrose's sermons. As a teacher of rhetoric, Augustine admired Ambrose's style but particularly the content. Ambrose often modeled his sermons on Cicero and he frequently quoted some of the pagan philosophers. At the same time as he listened to Ambrose, Augustine was studying the New Testament, especially the letters of St. Paul.

Augustine's *Confessions* details the struggle he was having with his faith by this time. On the matter of chastity, for example, he prayed, "Give me chastity, but not yet." He admitted that he was afraid God "would hear me too soon, and heal me of the disease which I wished to have satisfied rather than cured."

As Augustine's struggle continued, Monica convinced him to end his relationship with his mistress and to send her back to North Africa. Adeodatus, now nine, remained with his father and grandmother in Milan.

Finally the day arrived when the struggle

became too much for Augustine. He says that he threw himself under a fig tree. While he lay there despairing, he heard a childlike voice repeating "*Tolle lege! Tolle lege!*" (Take, read! Take, read!). He took up the Bible and read the first thing that came to his eyes, from St. Paul's Epistles: "Not in revelry and drunkenness, not in debauchery and wantonness, not in strife and jealousy. But put on the Lord Jesus Christ, and as for the flesh, take no thought for its lusts."

His struggle was over, and he hurried into the house and told Monica. He wrote. "Thence we go in to my mother; we tell her; she rejoices; we related in order how it took place; she leaps for joy, and triumphs, and blessed Thee; for she perceived that Thou had given her more for me than she was wont to beg by her pitiful and most sorrowful groanings.... And Thou didst convert her mourning into joy."

Augustine was baptized by Ambrose on Holy Saturday of the year 387, along with his son Adeodatus. He then resolved to return to North Africa, so he, Monica, Adeodatus, Navigius and some friends traveled to the Italian port city of Ostia. There one day, while waiting for a ship to take them to Africa, Monica and Augustine were leaning on a window sill looking out over a garden. During their pleasant conversation, Monica said to Augustine, "Son, for my own part I have no further delight in anything in this life. What I do here any longer; and to what end I am here, I know not, now that my hopes in this world are accomplished. One thing there was for which I desired to linger for a while in this life, that I might see you a Catholic Christian before I died. My God has done this for me more abundantly, that I should now see you, despising earthly happiness, become His servant. Why am I still here?"

Augustine relates that five days later Monica fell sick of a fever, which turned into a coma. She recovered once, but told Augustine and Navigius, "Here you will bury your mother." Navigius said something about wishing that she would not die in a strange place but in her own land, and Augustine too remembered that she once spoke about being buried next to her husband. She had, in fact, made such arrangements in Tagaste. As Augustine wrote, "For because they had lived in great harmony together, she also wished to have this addition to that happiness, and to have it remembered among men, that after her pilgrimage beyond the seas, what was earthly of this united pair had been permitted to be united beneath the same earth."

Augustine learned, though, that, when he was absent one day, Monica had told some of his friends that she didn't care where she was buried. She told them, "Nothing is far to God; nor was it to be feared lest at the end of the world, He should not recognize where He were to raise me up."

Monica died on the ninth day of her illness, when she was 56 and Augustine 33. As she died, Adeodatus burst into a loud wail and, of course, everybody else felt the sadness of separation. However, Augustine wrote, "We thought it not fitting to solemnize that funeral with tearful lament and groanings, for thereby do they for the most part express grief for the departed, as though unhappy or altogether dead; whereas she was neither unhappy in her death nor altogether dead." Later, though, his grief overflowed and he gave way to tears for a mother "who had for many years wept for me that I might live in Thine eyes."

Augustine devotes several pages of his *Confessions* to reflections on his mother's godly life and all that he owed to her. He ends with a prayer that "she rest then in peace with the husband before and after whom she had never any; whom she obeyed, with patience bringing forth fruit unto Thee, that she might win him also unto Thee."

After Monica's death, Augustine did not continue on to North Africa immediately. Rather he went to Rome, where he spoke out against the Manichaeans. A year passed before he went back to North Africa, where he lived in his own home in Tagaste. Here Adeodatus died when he was only 17.

Augustine went on to become a priest at age 36 and then bishop when he was 41. He continued as Bishop of Hippo for 35 years, becoming the most influential ecclesiastical figure not only of the fifth century but for many centuries thereafter.

The Church celebrates St. Monica's feast on August 27, the day before St. Augustine's feast.

ST. LOUIS

S t. Louis was the king of France during the 13th century. As is true of any other rank, there have been good kings and bad kings. Louis IX was a good king, an exemplary man, but also the product of his times. He was also a faithful husband and the father of 11 children, five sons and six daughters.

Louis was born on April 25, 1214. His father was King Louis VIII and his mother was Queen Blanche, daughter of Alfonso of Castile and Eleanor of England. His mother carefully supervised his education. Naturally, he had tutors who schooled him in Latin, how to speak in public and write carefully, and in the military arts and government. But Blanche was particularly careful about his education in spiritual matters. She is said to have told him often as he was growing up, "I love you, my dear son, as much as a mother can love her child; but I would rather see you dead at my feet than that you should commit a mortal sin."

His biographer, the Sieur de Joinville, says

that Louis never forgot that. After he was an adult, Louis once asked Joinville, "Would you rather be a leper or commit a mortal sin?" Considering the wretched lives lepers lived in Europe at that time, Joinville replied, "I would rather commit 30 mortal sins than be a leper!" Louis, though, told him, "When a man dies, he is healed of leprosy in his body; but when a man who has committed a mortal sin dies he cannot know of a certainty that he has in his lifetime repented in such sort that God has forgiven him; wherefore he must stand in great fear lest that leprosy of sin last as long as God is in Paradise."

Louis VIII didn't inherit the throne until Louis IX was eight years old and he died when Louis was only 12. Louis IX was crowned king in 1226 but Queen Blanche was declared regent until Louis came of age. This was the signal for some of the country's barons to try to seize power, but Blanche was adept at forging alliances and overcoming rebels on the battlefield. When Louis assumed control in 1235, his position was strong.

When he was barely 20, Louis married Margaret, the oldest daughter of Raymond Beranger, Count of Provence. Margaret's sister, Eleanor, married King Henry III of England; another sister, Sanchia, married Henry's brother, Richard of Cornwall; and still another sister, Beatrice, married Louis' brother Charles. Royalty married royalty in those days as a way of forging political alliances.

The line of French kings descended from Louis IX continued all the way to 1793, when King Louis XVI was killed by the guillotine during the French Revolution.

Louis IX supported and promoted the Catholic Church's Religious Orders. One of his first acts as king was to built the monastery of Royaumont. He also installed the Carthusians in the palace of Vauvert in Paris and helped his mother found the convent of Maubuisson.

This was an era when relics of Christ and the saints were venerated with great devotion. One of the relics Louis was offered was the Crown of Thorns with which Christ was crowned at the time of his crucifixion. He bought the crown from the Eastern Emperor of Constantinople. To house it he built the exquisite Gothic Shrine of Sainte-Chapelle on the island in the Seine River named for him. Since the French Revolution, the shrine has been empty.

Louis was devout. He not only attended Mass daily, he attended two Masses daily. He kept priests near him to chant the Liturgy of the Hours. He forbade any celebrations at court that might be dangerous to morals and he allowed no obscenity or profanity. He could, however, carry his beliefs to extremes. For example, he issued an edict that anyone guilty of blasphemy was to be branded. Later, on the advice of Pope Clement IV, this penalty was reduced to a fine, flogging or imprisonment.

In 1230, Louis forbade all forms of usury, in accordance with the Church's teachings. Money-lenders whose profits were deemed exorbitant were exacted a contribution toward the crusade the pope was then trying to launch.

In 1242, the Count of La Marche, Hugh of Lusignan, made trouble for the king. Hugh's wife, Isabel, was the widow of King John and the mother of King Henry III of England, who crossed the English Channel to help his stepfather. Louis' army was able to defeat the rebels and Henry fled back to England.

In 1244, Louis, when he was 30, announced that he was going to lead a crusade against the Muslim Saracens in the Holy Land. Innocent IV was pope at the time and he, as did his predecessors, encouraged crusades to free the Holy Land from the "infidels." There were eight major crusades between 1095 and 1270. Most of those who fought in the crusades did so for religious and spiritual reasons and several popes promised nothing less than eternal life in heaven to all those who participated. It must be said, though, that many of the crusaders were ruthless men who massacred men, women and children when they conquered cities.

Louis led two crusades, the final two. Although he announced his first crusade in 1244, he didn't actually leave until June 12, 1248. Elaborate preparations were made before he left, including the naming of his mother as regent in his absence and raising money to support the crusade. The Ecumenical Council of Lyons in 1245 taxed all benefices a twentieth of their income for three years for relief of the Holy Land, much to the chagrin of the English representatives at the council.

The first objective of the crusade was to defeat the Sultan of Egypt, Melek Selah, who controlled Palestine. Louis, accompanied by his wife and three brothers, led his troops to Damietta, at the mouth of one of the branches of the Nile River. The city was taken easily and Louis and his queen made a solemn but humble entry into the defeated city, walking barefoot and singing the *Te Deum*.

Louis proved to be a merciful conqueror. He issued orders that all acts of violence committed by his soldiers should be punished and restitution made to the persons injured. He forbade the killing of any Muslims taken prisoner and gave directions that any of them who wanted to become Christians should be given instructions and baptized.

The conquest of Damietta, though, was Louis' only victory. The rising of the Nile and the summer heat made it impossible to follow up his success. Queen Margaret was sent back to Paris. Finally, in the fall of 1249, six months after the conquest of Damietta, Louis' troops advanced across the river and started a long battle against the Saracens. The ranks of the crusaders were thinned by disease as well as by combat and in April of

1250 Louis himself, weakened with dysentery, was taken prisoner. Most of his army was slaughtered.

Louis was a strange prisoner. Even during his captivity, he recited the Liturgy of the Hours with his two chaplains as if he were in his own palace, and he had the prayers of the Mass read to him every day. When he was insulted by his guards, he assumed an air of majesty and authority. In the course of negotiations for his release, the Mamluk emirs overthrew and murdered the sultan. Louis and his fellow prisoners were released, although the sick and wounded crusaders still in Damietta were killed.

Louis and what was left of his army sailed for Palestine, where he stayed until 1254, fortifying the cities of Acre, Jaffa, Caesarea and Tyre, all along the Mediterranean coast. He visited the Holy Places that still remained in Christian hands. In 1254, his mother died and Louis returned to France. He had been gone for six years and he continued to wear a cross on his shoulder to indicate his intention of returning. He didn't do so, though, for 16 years.

Back in Paris, Louis resumed his duties as king. He laid the foundations for the famous college of theology known as the Sorbonne, appointing as its head his own confessor, Father Robert de Sorbon. Louis secured approval for the college from Pope Clement IV. Louis also founded the hospital known as Quinze-vingt (fifteen-twenty), so-called because it had beds for 300 patients.

Louis practiced personal charity on a daily basis. Every day he had 13 special guests from among the poor to eat with him and he saw that a large number of poor were fed. In Lent and Advent he personally helped serve all the poor who presented themselves. He visited the sick on a regular basis and even cared for people with leprosy. Because of his care for the poor and the sick, he is one of the patrons of the Third Order of St. Francis.

He also had a particular passion for justice. He used to sit in his palace or under a large oak tree in the forest of Vincennes and listen to any of his subjects who came with grievances. He gave what seemed to be wise and impartial judgments. He replaced the feudal method of settling disputes by combat with peaceful arbitration or the judicial process of trial. Centuries later, whenever the French people complained of oppression, they cried for justice as it had been during the reign of Louis IX.

His sense of justice extended to nations. France was frequently at war with England and Spain. In 1258 Louis concluded the Peace of Paris with his old enemy, Henry III of England. Hoping to preserve peace, he voluntarily surrendered to England the French provinces of Limousin, Quercy and Perigord while Henry renounced all claim to Normandy, Anjou, Maine, Touraine, and Poitou.

France's nobles were outraged by Louis' concessions, since France had won the battles against
England, but the king said that he hoped to achieve
a lasting friendship between the two nations. Unfortunately, after Louis' death, that didn't happen.
The Hundred Years' War between the two countries was to last from 1337 to 1453.

Louis also tried to cement good relations with
Spain by making concessions to the King of Aragon, giving up claims to Roussillon and Barcelona.

In 1267 Louis announced that he was going
to lead another crusade. His people objected, fear-
ing that they would lose the king they revered, but
Pope Clement IV supported the crusade and
granted Louis one-tenth of all Church revenues to
meet the expenses. Louis appointed the abbot of
St. Denis and Simon de Clermont as regents in his
absence and took his three oldest sons with him.

The troops left on July 1, 1270, headed for
Tunisia. Louis had been told that the emir in Tunis
was ready to be converted and join the crusade.
The information was false, as Louis learned to his
dismay when he landed at Carthage. Since he
didn't have the support he expected, he decided
to wait in Carthage until the King of Sicily could
send troops. Dysentery again broke out and among
the victims was Louis' second son, John, who had
been born at Damietta during the earlier crusade.

On the day that John died, Louis also caught
the disease. When he realized that he was dying,

Louis called his eldest son Philip, to whom he gave his last instructions, written, it is said, in his own hand. Those instructions deserve to be quoted in full because they demonstrate a saintly father's concern for the spiritual well being of his son. Here they are:

"Fair son, the first thing I would teach you is to set your heart to love God; for unless he love God none can be saved. Keep yourself from doing anything that is displeasing to God, that is to say, from mortal sin. Contrariwise, you should suffer every manner of torment rather than commit a mortal sin.

"If God send you adversity, receive it in patience and give thanks to our Savior and think yourself that you have deserved it, and that He will make it turn to your advantage. If He send you prosperity, then thank Him humbly, so that you become not worse from pride or any other cause, when you ought to be better. For we should not fight against God with His own gifts.

"Confess yourself often and choose for your confessor a right worthy man who knows how to teach you what to do, and what not to do; and bear yourself in such sort that your confessor and your friends shall dare to reprove you for your misdoings. Listen to the services of Holy Church devoutly, and without chattering; and pray to God with your heart and with your lips, and especially at Mass when the consecration takes place. Let your heart be tender and full of pity toward those who are poor, miserable, and afflicted, and comfort and help them to the utmost of your power.

"Maintain the good customs of your realm and abolish the bad. Be not covetous against your people and do not burden them with taxes and imposts save when you are in great need.

"If you have any great burden weighing upon your heart, tell it to your confessor or to some right worthy man who is not full of vain words. You shall be able to bear it more easily.

"See that you have in your company men, whether religious or lay, who are right worthy and loyal and not full of covetousness, and confer with them often; and fly and eschew the company of the wicked. Hearken willingly to the word of God and keep it in your heart, and seek diligently after prayers and indulgences. Love all that is good and profitable and hate all that is evil, wherever it may be.

"Let none be so bold as to say before you any word that would draw or move to sin, or so bold as to speak evil behind another's back for pleasure's sake; nor do you suffer any word in disparagement of God and of His saints to be spoken in your presence. Give often thanks to God for all the good things He has bestowed on you, so that you be accounted worthy to receive more.

"In order to do justice and right to your subjects, be upright and firm, turning neither to the right hand nor to the left, but always to what is just; and do maintain the cause of the poor until such a time as the truth is made clear. And if anyone has an action against you, make full inquiry until you know the truth; for thus shall your counselors judge the more boldly according to the truth, whether for you or against.

"If you hold something that belongs to another, whether by your own act or the act of your predecessors, and the matter is certain, make restitution without delay. If the matter is doubtful, cause inquiry to be made by wise men diligently and promptly.

"Give heed that your servants and your subjects live under you in peace and uprightness. Especially maintain the good cities and commons of your realm in the same estate and with the same franchises as they enjoyed under your predecessors; and if there be something to amend, amend and set it right, and keep them in your favor and love. For because of the power and wealth of the great cities, your own subjects, and especially your peers and your barons and foreigners also will fear to undertake something against you.

"Love and honor all persons belonging to Holy Church, and see that no one take away or diminish the gifts and alms paid to them by your predecessors. It is related of King Philip, my grandfather, that one of his counselors once told him that those of Holy Church did him much harm and damage in that they deprived him of his rights, and diminished his jurisdiction, and that it was a great marvel that he suffered it; and the good king replied that he believed this might well be so, but he had regard to the benefits and courtesies that God had bestowed on him, and so thought it better to abandon some of his rights than to have any contention with the people of Holy Church.

"To your father and mother you shall give honor and reverence, and you shall obey their commandments. Bestow the benefices of Holy Church on persons who are righteous and of a clean life, and do it on the advice of men of worth and uprightness.

"Beware of undertaking a war against any Christian prince without great deliberation; and if it has to be undertaken, see that you do no hurt to Holy Church and to those that have done you no injury. If wars and dissensions arise among your subjects, see that you appease them as soon as you are able.

"Use diligence to have good provosts and bailiffs, and inquire often of them and of those of your household how they conduct themselves, and if there be found in them any vice or inordinate covetousness or falsehood or trickery. Labor to free your land from all vile iniquity, and especially strike down with all your power evil swearing and heresy. See to it that the expense of your household be reasonable.

"Finally, my very dear son, cause Masses to

be sung for my soul, and prayer to be said throughout your realm; and give to me a special share and full part in all the good you do. Fair, dear son, I give you all the blessings that a good father can give to his son. And may the Blessed Trinity and all the saints keep and defend you from all evils; and God give you grace to do His will always, so that He be honored in you, and that you and I may both, after this mortal life is ended, be with Him together and praise Him everlastingly. Amen."

On August 24, Louis received the last sacraments. He lost his speech the next day from 9 till 12 o'clock. Then, regaining his speech, he prayed, "Lord, I will enter into Thine house; I will worship in Thy holy temple and give glory to Thy name." At 3 o'clock, he spoke again, "Into Thy hands I commend my soul," and immediately died. He was 56.

His bones and heart were taken back to France where they were enshrined in the abbey-church of St. Denis. They remained there until the French Revolution, when they were scattered.

Louis was canonized in 1297, 27 years after his death. His feast is observed on August 25.

ST. FRANCES OF ROME

S t. Frances of Rome was one of the Church's
great mystics as well as a devoted wife and
mother. God has granted to some people the
gifts of mysticism, marvelous visions and amazing
miracles, but He seems to combine these gifts with
suffering, too. This was true of Frances.

Rome was not an easy city in which to live
when Frances was born there in 1384. What is
known as the Great Western Schism, which divided
the Church, began four years earlier and would
continue until 1417. Two men — later three —
claimed the papacy. Adherents of the claimants
fought fiercely, sometimes pitting one Italian city
against another. And various pestilences were common occurrences in those days.

Frances was born in the Trastevere (across
the Tiber) district of Rome to Paul Busso and
Jacobella dei Roffredeschi, both of whom were of
noble birth. She grew up in the midst of luxury
but also in a pious family. Soon after she was born,
she was baptized in the Church of St. Agnes on

the Piazza Navona, receiving the feminine form of the revered saint from Assisi as her name.

Frances was undoubtedly different from the other children around her. From a very early age, she liked to spend time in solitude, taking no interest in childish games. She spent her time in prayer almost as soon as she learned to speak and she accompanied her mother to daily Mass in one of the many churches in the neighborhood. Soon her mother's confessor, Benedictine Father Antonello, became her confessor too.

When Frances was 11 years old, Father Antonello allowed her to take a vow of virginity because she told him that she wanted to become a nun. When she told her parents, though, she was met with point-blank refusal; they insisted that she was to be married. In fact, her future husband had already been selected. Heartbroken, the little girl went back to her confessor. Father Antonello counseled her that marriage might be God's will for her and said that she could easily be dispensed from her vow. Frances returned to her father and consented to the marriage.

It is certainly shocking to us that a girl could be married before she was even 12 years old, but this was in keeping with the customs of the time. So in 1395 Frances was married to Lorenzo de Ponziano. The marriage was a happy one in every respect. Unlike the husbands of some married saints, Lorenzo was as virtuous and talented as he was rich and was happy that his wife was a holy woman.

However, not surprisingly, it took a while for a 12-year-old to adjust to her new life in her husband's home. She had to learn to please not only her husband but also her parents-in-law. But she soon found a soul-sister in Vannozza, the wife of Lorenzo's older brother, Paluzzo. Vannozza found Frances weeping bitterly one day and confided to her that she, too, had preferred a life of retirement and prayer to that of a noblewoman in Rome but that she had found happiness in doing God's will in the married life. It was the beginning of a close friendship that was to last for more than 30 years as these two saintly women consoled and helped each other, and prayed together. With their husbands' blessings, these two women set out to visit the poor of Rome. They visited the hospital of Santo Spirito near the Vatican daily to nurse the patients, singling out those suffering from the most repellent diseases.

While she was doing that, though, Frances willingly fulfilled all the social obligations attached to her, and her husband's, status in Rome. She wore fine clothes and splendid jewelry, but under those clothes she wore a hairshirt as a form of penance. Naturally, some of the people in their circle of friends told Lorenzo that he ought to stop his wife's "eccentricities," but he paid no attention to them.

About a year after their marriage, Frances became seriously ill and it appeared that she would not survive. Her family was filled with grief, especially her father who now blamed himself for having refused her request to become a nun. But Frances herself remained calm and resigned to God's will. For a time she rallied, but then became much worse and it seemed that she was about to die.

Then occurred one of those marvels which were to become more and more frequent in her later years. As she lay on her sickbed, suddenly her room was filled with brilliant light and a man appeared in pilgrim garb that shone like gold. He told her, "I am St. Alexis. God has sent me to you, faithful servant of Christ, that I might cure you of your illness." He then spread his mantle over her. Frances was cured immediately. Hurrying to her sister-in-law Vannozza, she told her what had happened. At daybreak, the two women slipped out of the house, attended Mass at the Church of Santa Maria Nuova, and then went to the Church of St. Alexis, where they venerated his relics and thanked him for the cure.

After that episode, Frances and Vannozza lived even more austere lives than they had previously. Lorenzo built a little hut for them in the rear of their garden and here they prayed together and did penance without being seen by the rest of the household. They continued their daily routine of assisting the poor and nursing the sick.

Frances and Lorenzo seem to have had six children, but we know about only three of them; the other three apparently died during infancy. Her first child, Giovanni Battista (John the Baptist) was born when Frances was 16 in 1400. Giovanni Evangelista (John the Evangelist) was born in 1403 and Agnes in 1408. After the children were born, Frances spent less time with the poor and the sick because she allowed no one but herself to take care of the children during their childhood.

When Frances was 17, her mother in law, Cecilia, died. Her father-in-law, Andrew, asked Frances to become mistress of the household and in full charge of the De Ponziani palace. Frances protested that Vannozza, the wife of the elder brother, should have this position, but both Andrew and Vannozza insisted that Frances was more suitable for the tasks. She discharged her duties efficiently, treating the servants as brothers and sisters. Andrew and Lorenzo gave her a free hand in dispensing food, clothing and money to the poor, so she gave orders that no poor people were ever to be sent away without giving them something in charity.

Then one year Rome was stricken with a severe famine. Frances was giving away so much food and wine that Andrew, her father-in-law, decided that it was too much. He locked the door of the cellar where the supplies were kept. Frances and Vannozza simply went about the city begging for food for the poor. Whatever they were able to get from begging was miraculously multiplied by God and the two women continued to feed all the poor who came to their door. Andrew, thinking that the women were continuing to distribute the family's food against his wishes, rebuked his sons for having disobedient wives. But Frances told him to open the cellar and see that she had not taken any of his supplies. When he did so, he found more grain and wine than had been stored there originally. He apologized to his daughters-in-law and told his friends what had happened. Soon the miracle was known all over Rome.

In 1408, the fortunes of the Ponziani family changed drastically. During the dispute over who was the legitimate pope, the troops of Ladislaus of Naples had entered Rome. Ladislaus supported the antipope, Benedict XIII. Lorenzo was an officer in the papal army of Pope Gregory XII. During one of the battles between the forces of both sides, Lorenzo was stabbed and carried home near death. Frances' experience nursing the sick in hospitals now stood her in good stead and, contrary to expectations, Lorenzo recovered. He then went into hiding.

Count Troja, who had been appointed governor of Rome by Ladislaus of Naples, took vengeance on the supporters of Pope Gregory. His soldiers pillaged Frances' home, arrested Paluzzo

(Vannozza's husband), and demanded little Battista as a hostage. Battista was taken away but, while Frances was praying in the Church of Ara Coeli on the Capitoline Hill, he was released in circumstances that seemed to be miraculous.

In 1410, while the cardinals were assembled in Bologna to elect a new pope to try to settle the schism, Ladislaus again seized Rome. Lorenzo once again was able to go into hiding but the Ponziani palace was again plundered and Battista was again taken captive. In the Campagna, where the Ponziani family owned large estates, their properties were destroyed, flocks slaughtered, and many peasants murdered. Somehow Battista was again able to escape and he joined his father, but Frances had to live in a corner of her ruined home with Evangelista, Agnes and Vannozza, whose husband was still a prisoner. The two women continued to try to relieve the sufferings of their neighbors.

These were very difficult years for the citizens of Rome as they suffered from the devastation of war, from famine and pestilence. As Frances and Vannozza went around the city assisting the poor and the sick, God gave Frances the gift of healing. Many people whom the doctors had given up on were restored to health through her prayers.

The Great Western Schism continued until the Council of Constance was convened in 1414. It was to continue until 1417, but in 1414 the Ponziani were able to regain their property and

Lorenzo was able to return to Rome. He was a broken man, however, and had to be cared for by Frances until his death.

But before Frances could be reunited with Lorenzo and Battista, her other two children died. First it was eight-year-old Evangelista, who died in 1411 during one of the pestilences that were common in Rome. After his death, Frances turned part of her house into a hospital.

Two years after Evangelista's death, Frances had a vision. Evangelista appeared to her with a young man in brilliant garments. Frances tried to embrace Evangelista but felt nothing when she touched him. Then Evangelista told her, "Do not mourn for us who are in heaven. We have no pain or sorrow, but enjoy unspeakable bliss, as we gaze on the infinite goodness of God and praise His adorable majesty. My sister Agnes will soon join me in glory. But God has sent you this archangel to comfort you."

The words that Frances heard in her vision soon came true. Little five-year-old Agnes began to fail and soon died.

The biographies of St. Frances contain numerous stories of her visions. They also tell us that she was always aware of the presence of her guardian angel. In fact, she could see her guardian angel — and feel him. If she didn't follow his instructions, she received a slap on the face from him, a slap that others testified they could hear, although they couldn't see anyone except Frances.

After the vision announcing Agnes' approaching death, Frances' guardian angel was replaced by the special archangel whom Evangelista introduced. That archangel remained with Frances for 23 years and then was succeeded toward the end of her life by an angel of even higher dignity — one of the angelic spirits known as Powers. From this angel she had sublime visions of heaven, hell and purgatory.

In 1417 Frances again became seriously ill. Grief over the deaths of her children, her labors for the poor and her austerities seemed to have taken their toll. Once again, Frances remained calm and always gentle with those around her. Eventually she recovered her health

In 1418, when Battista was 18, Lorenzo arranged a marriage for him with a girl named Mobilia. Frances took her into the household with love, but that love was not reciprocated. Mobilia ridiculed Frances, saying, "How can anyone feel respect for a woman who thinks of nothing but the poor, and dresses like one of them, and goes about the streets carrying wood and old clothes to them?"

Frances knew that Mobilia was ridiculing her, but she continued to treat her kindly and prayed for her. One day Mobilia was ranting and raving about her mother-in-law when she suddenly began to tremble and fell into a faint. When she came to, she found Frances caring for her. Feeling ashamed, she asked Frances for her forgiveness, which of course was given immediately. Mobilia changed her attitude and her love for Frances increased. She even kept a notebook on Frances and it was used in Frances' canonization process. Eventually, Mobilia took over the management of the De Ponziani palace, leaving Frances free to devote her efforts to the sick and the poor.

By this time, knowledge of Frances' work, and her miracles, had spread throughout Rome. People in need flocked to her and no one left her without being consoled. She began to visit other Roman hospitals and to seek out the sick in their homes. She often took home the clothes of the sick, washed them and mended them, and then took them back to the sick. She also sent priests to the sick to provide for their spiritual needs. In time, she supported, at her own expense, a priest who would go to the hospitals and visit the sick whom she designated.

Soon other women, admirers, began to imitate her devout and charitable way of life and would accompany her on her journeys to the sick and the poor (Vannozza had already died by this time). Finally, under the guidance of Father Antonello, Frances drew up a few simple rules for these women, organizing them into a religious society. They were to continue to live in the world and would take no vows, but they would pledge to make a simple offering of themselves to God and to serve the poor. Father Antonello affiliated the society with the Benedictines of Monte Oliveto, to which he belonged. They were known as the Oblates of Mount Olivet.

The society continued that way for seven years. Then, after Frances had another marvelous vision during which St. Peter told her that it was God's will that the women should live in community, she changed the rules. Frances found a small house at the Tor dei Specchi ("Tower of Mirrors") and, on March 25, 1434 (the feast of the Annunciation), the first 10 Oblates of Mount Olivet took up their residence there.

Today, when we are accustomed to many Religious Orders, it's difficult to understand how innovative the Oblates were. During the 15th century, a woman could be either a cloistered nun or she remained "in the world." There were no women religious who lived in community but who devoted themselves to charitable works, such as teaching or nursing. Nevertheless, Frances' convent and congregation received the approval of the pope the year after it was founded.

Frances, though, remained in her home where she continued to care for Lorenzo, whose health was failing. She refused to allow herself to be called the foundress of the Oblates and insisted that all members of the congregation be subject to its first superior, Agnes de Selli.

Then, in 1436, a little more than 40 years after Frances had married Lorenzo, he died a holy death. He was laid to rest beside Evangelista and Agnes. Now Frances felt free to leave her home and to request admission to the convent of Tor dei Specchi. She asked to be taken in as a simple and humble suppliant, but the other Sisters insisted that she become their superior. At first she refused and it wasn't until months later, out of obedience to her confessor, that she accepted the superiorship of the community. She used her privileges as superior to habitually assign herself the most menial tasks.

Frances was to live only four years at Tor dei Specchi. She used those years to increase her penances. She ate only one meal a day, some bread and vegetables in the evening. All her life she had worn her hairshirt but now she wore a chain with sharp points around her waist, under the hairshirt. She indulged in the type of self-inflicted penances that were common among holy people of that time but which might be more for admiration than emulation.

Her confessor for most of her life, Father Antonello, died and she took as her new confessor Father Mattiotti. This man drew up a long account of Frances' visions and miracles that later were used during the process of her beatification and canonization. Only a couple will be mentioned here.

One day it was discovered that the bread in the convent was enough for only three people. Frances blessed it and distributed it to 15 Sisters until they all had as much as they could eat, with plenty left over for the next day.

On another occasion, the Sisters were gathering wood for the poor, as was their custom, when one of the Sisters complained of being hungry and thirsty. Frances told the Sisters to go to a nearby vineyard and gather grapes for themselves. Despite the fact that it was the middle of January and the vines should have been nothing but sticks, the Sisters found them full of grapes.

One day in March of 1440, Frances was notified that her son, Battista, was very ill. She hurried to him in her former home and had been there for only a short time when Battista felt much better. He got up from his bed, miraculously cured. However, it soon became obvious that Frances had given her life for his. As she was getting up to return to the convent, she was suddenly stricken with either a heart attack or a stroke. She tried to walk back to the convent, but she could not, and she was carried back to her former home.

She lingered there for seven days before she died. Her last words, spoken to Father Mattiotti, were, "The heavens are open and the angels descend. My archangel has finished his task. He stands before me and beckons me to follow him." As she died at age 56 on March 9, 1440 her face, which had shown the effects of her age and suffering, suddenly took on the radiance of youth and beauty.

She was buried in the church she loved so much, Santa Maria Nuova, which is now known as the Church of Santa Francesca Romana, St. Frances of Rome.

The people of Rome took her canonization for granted. However, with the continuing crises in the Church at the time, the process of her cause was delayed. Finally, on May 29, 1608, 168 years after her death, Pope Paul V declared her a saint. Her feast day is celebrated on March 9, the date of her death.

ST. ELIZABETH OF HUNGARY

S t. Elizabeth of Hungary's spiritual director,
Conrad of Marburg, wrote that he had seldom seen a more contemplative woman. He
wrote, "When she was coming from private prayer,
some religious men and women often saw her face
shining marvelously and light coming from her
eyes like the rays of the sun."

But St. Elizabeth wasn't known primarily for
her contemplative nature. She was known, above
all, for her generosity and care for the sick and
the poor. She used to visit the sick twice a day, in
the morning and in the evening. She paid particular attention to those whom others didn't want to
care for because of their repulsive nature. She gave
food and clothing to the poor and performed many
other kindly services.

Because of these charitable activities, St.
Elizabeth of Hungary is the patroness of Catholic
Charities and of tertiaries (lay people in Religious
Orders), especially the Secular Franciscans.

She was the daughter of the king of Hungary,

Andrew II, who reigned from 1205 to 1235. Andrew went down in history for impoverishing his country by reckless expenditures. His nobles eventually forced him to make concessions in the Golden Bull, published seven years after the signing of the Magna Carta in England.

That really had nothing to do with Elizabeth, though, who was born in Hungary in 1207. From her earliest childhood years, she rejected the life of luxury she could have lived and chose instead a life of penance and asceticism.

When she was 14 she was married to Ludvig IV of Thuringia (a German principality). Although the marriage was arranged by her parents, the couple grew to love each other immensely. They had three children in the six years before Ludvig's death.

Ludvig heartily approved of Elizabeth's charitable work. After her marriage, her almsgiving increased since she now had the revenue from four principalities. She ordered that one of her castles be converted into a hospital and she sold her luxurious possessions and rich clothes for the sake of the poor. She wore simple clothing and daily took bread to the hundreds of people who begged at her doors. She made it her life's work to try to relieve the plight of the poor.

Then Ludvig went off to fight in the Fifth Crusade, led by Emperor Frederick II. While he was gone, he died, although not in battle. Eliza-

beth, of course, was heartbroken. Ludvig's death
also meant the end of Elizabeth's ability to give
generously to the poor because her husband's family looked on her as squandering the royal purse.
Eventually, they threw her out of the Wartburg
palace. Then, according to Conrad of Marburg,
"she sought the highest perfection; filled with tears,
she implored me to let her beg for alms from door
to door."

In 1229, Ludvig's allies returned from the
Crusades and reinstated Elizabeth, since her son
was the legal heir to the throne. But before that
happened, in 1228, Elizabeth joined the Third
Order of St. Francis. After making arrangements
for the care of her children by others, on Good
Friday of that year, she laid her hands on the altar
in a chapel and renounced all her worldly possessions. Then, according to Conrad of Marburg,
"Against my will she followed me to Marburg. Here
in the town she built a hospice where she gathered together the weak and the feeble. There she
attended the most wretched and contemptible at
her own table."

It's interesting that Conrad said "against my
will" because some of Elizabeth's biographers
thought that he had too much control over Elizabeth. In her book *The Directory of Saints*, Annette
Sandoval says that Elizabeth "was counseled by a
tyrant named Conrad of Marburg. He was insistent that she suffer extreme deprivation and hu-

mility for the rest of her short life, which ended at the tender age of 23."

Whether or not Conrad was a "tyrant," it is true that Elizabeth died before her 24th birthday in 1231. From 1228 to 1231 she continued to care for the poor and the sick in the hospice in Marburg, which she founded in honor of St. Francis, who was canonized in 1228 after dying in 1226.

Her spiritual director, Conrad, was with her when she died. Here is his description of her death: "I heard her confession. When I asked what should be done about her goods and possessions, she replied that anything which seemed to be hers belonged to the poor. She asked me to distribute everything except one worn out dress in which she wished to be buried. When all this had been decided, she received the body of Our Lord. Afterward, until vespers, she spoke often of the holiest things she had heard in sermons. Then, she devoutly commended to God all who were sitting near by, and as if falling into a gentle sleep, she died."

Because of her great popularity, she was canonized four years later, in 1235. Her feast day is celebrated on November 17.

ST. ELIZABETH OF PORTUGAL

The most popular name for a married saint obviously is Elizabeth. In this book we have chapters on Sts. Elizabeth Ann Seton, Elizabeth the wife of Zachary, Elizabeth of Hungary and Elizabeth of Portugal. By contrast, there are no duplicate names among the married men in this book.

St. Elizabeth of Portugal was related to another St. Elizabeth. Her great-aunt was St. Elizabeth of Hungary. If, after reading about both of these saints, the reader confuses some details of their lives, it will be understandable. They led similar lives even though Elizabeth of Portugal was born 64 years after Elizabeth of Hungary.

Elizabeth of Portugal was born in 1271, not in Portugal but in Spain. She was the daughter of Pedro III, the future king of Aragon. She was named after St. Elizabeth of Hungary, but was actually called Isabella, the Spanish equivalent of the name. At her birth, her father became reconciled with his father James, the monarch who reigned in Aragon for 63 years. The reconciliation was a portent of things to come in Elizabeth's life.

Elizabeth learned self-discipline early in the court of her parents, and she quickly developed a taste for the spiritual. At the early age of 12, she was given in marriage to Denis, king of Portugal. It was a political marriage, of course, as most marriages among kings and queens were in those days, but no one could have been a better wife to Denis than Elizabeth.

In Spain and Portugal, the 13th and 14th centuries were marked by wars to acquire or to retain territory, by domestic struggles between crown and nobility, and by constant intrigues. This was the atmosphere in which Elizabeth grew up. In Spain in 1282, when she was 11, her father seized Sicily from the House of Anjou. For this act Pedro III was excommunicated by Pope Martin IV. Pedro died in 1285, but by this time Elizabeth was married to Denis of Portugal.

In Portugal, the 13th century witnessed violent disputes between kings and bishops. The pope had tried to depose Denis' predecessor, Alfonso III, but unsuccessfully. Seeing the need for moral and religious reform, the Franciscans and Dominicans entered Portugal to try to start a spiritual revival, but they were expelled from Oporto by the bishop of that city. However, by their fervor and austerity of life, these missionaries were able to win the friendship of the people and founded many monasteries.

This was the situation when Elizabeth arrived in Portugal as Denis' wife. Through her influence, Denis was able to bring the contest between Church and State to an end by the end of the 13th century. He renounced the royal right of appointment of benefices in 1284, a year after his marriage to Elizabeth, he restored the property seized under Alfonso III, and he promised to respect clerical privileges and the ancient laws and customs. He pursued a policy of decentralization which made the clergy and the military orders dependent upon the crown. Even at a young age, Elizabeth has been credited with influencing her husband to make some of these decisions.

The relationship between Elizabeth and Denis was a mixed one. On the one hand, he took her advice on political matters and about relations with the Church. On the other hand, his infidelity to her was a scandal to the entire kingdom. He fathered illegitimate children whom he seemed to favor over the children he had with Elizabeth.

Elizabeth and Denis had two children — Alfonso and Constance. Alfonso grew up very rebellious, undoubtedly at least partly because of the favor Denis seemed to give to his illegitimate sons. Twice Alfonso led troops against his father and twice Elizabeth had to bring about a reconciliation, actually riding a horse out between the opposing forces. She considered it her task to be a peacemaker.

During their married life, Denis gave Elizabeth full liberty to practice her daily devotions without feeling it necessary to participate with her. He admired Elizabeth's pious life, but didn't emulate it. So Elizabeth planned for herself a regular daily routine. She rose early in the morning in order to recite Matins, Lauds and Prime from the Liturgy of the Hours before attending Mass; she prayed Vespers in the afternoon and Compline before going to bed.

Her days included certain hours allotted to domestic affairs and public business as required of the wife of the king. But she also allotted time for works of charity. She gave orders to have pilgrims and poor strangers provided with lodging, and she visited the sick and the poor.

Elizabeth provided marriage dowries for poor girls and she founded various charitable establishments in the kingdom, especially a hospital in Coimbra, a house for penitent women at Torres Novas, and a refuge for foundlings.

But Elizabeth saw that her first responsibility was to try to bring peace to the Iberian Peninsula, not only in Portugal but also in Spain. She managed to stop or avert war between Ferdinand IV of Castile and his cousin and between that prince and her brother, James II of Aragon.

In 1324, Denis became seriously ill and Elizabeth gave all her attention to him, seldom leaving his room except to go to church. During his illness, Denis expressed sincere sorrow for his sinful life. He died on January 6, 1325.

After her husband's death, Elizabeth made a pilgrimage to Compostela and then expressed a wish to retire to a convent of Poor Clares which she had founded at Coimbra. She was dissuaded from doing that, though. Instead she was professed in the Third Order of St. Francis and moved to a house which she had built near the convent.

Her son Alfonso IV succeeded her husband as king of Portugal. He reigned from 1325 to 1357 and historians say that the prosperity of the country during his reign was due at least in part to Elizabeth's influence, which she exercised from her little house. This influence could be seen in Alfonso's agreement to resume the payment of tribute to the Holy See promised by one of his predecessors, Alfonso Henriquez, but not paid by Denis. Alfonso also tried to punish clerical misconduct, thus interfering in Church affairs. He tried to restore order in the Church in Portugal by appointing foreign prelates to positions of authority, an action that naturally aroused great opposition.

From her modest house in Coimbra, Elizabeth continued to try to be a peacemaker. Her daughter Constance was now married to King Alfonso XI of Castile, but there was bitter rivalry between him and Elizabeth's son, Alfonso IV of Portugal. In the summer of 1336, Elizabeth set out on a mission to try to bring lasting peace between

Castile and Portugal. It was a difficult journey, mainly because of the oppressive heat of the summer and the fact that Elizabeth was not well. When well-wishers tried to dissuade her from making the journey, she replied that there was no better way to give of her life and her health than by averting the miseries and destruction of war.

Her mission was successful, and peace was restored — at least for a while. But Elizabeth was worn out and she died on July 4, 1336. She was buried in the church of the Poor Clares monastery that she built in Coimbra.

St. Elizabeth of Portugal was canonized in 1626. Her feast day is celebrated on July 4.

ST. STEPHEN OF HUNGARY

S t. Stephen is both the first king and the patron saint of Hungary. He was the one who was primarily responsible for the Christianization of Hungary. He is also one of the canon ized saints who was married.

The 9th and 10th centuries saw much of Europe overrun by barbarian tribes such as the Huns, the Normans and the Bulgars. The tribe that overran Hungary was the Magyars. For centuries these people had wandered on the western confines of China but they also had a strong infusion of Hun and Turkish blood. In 885, under their chieftain Arpad, they began their permanent conquest of Hungary. Four years later they crossed the Alps into northern Italy. They also invaded Bavaria from 900 to 907, devastated Swabia in 913, southern Germany and Alsace in 917, and overwhelmed the Germans in 924.

The Magyars' advance was finally stopped in 933 when they were defeated at Gotha. But they returned in 943 to invade Italy again and they pillaged Burgundy in 955. Finally, they were decisively defeated by the united armies of Germany's Otto I in 955 and retreated back to Hungary. It seemed that Europe, having survived barbarian attacks from various places, could finally breathe again.

The Magyars still had control of Hungary. Here Prince Geza, the third ruler after Arpad, was shrewd enough to see the practical desirability of taking on Christianity as a protection against the inroads of his Christian neighbors. Situated where Hungary is, Geza had a choice of turning to the Eastern Church at Constantinople or to the Church of Rome. He chose Rome because he feared that, if he chose Eastern Christianity, his domain would be incorporated in the recently revived Eastern Empire.

Geza's first wife was Sarolta, one of the few Magyar women to be truly Christian. They had a son named Vaik, who was to become St. Stephen. Vaik was born in 975 and received careful early training from his mother. He had excellent Italian and Czech tutors in secular subjects and he also received a good grounding in Christianity.

Geza married a second time, this time to a Christian princess, Adelaide, sister of the duke of Poland. It was at her request that the Archbishop of Prague, Adalbert, came to Hungary on a preaching mission. During that mission, both Geza and Vaik were baptized. Vaik, 10 at the time, was given the name of the first Christian martyr, Stephen (Istvan in the Magyar language). A number of the Hungarian nobles were also baptized during Archbishop Adalbert's mission, but for most of them it was a conversion of expediency. Not so for Prince Stephen, whose entire mature life was spent spreading the faith and trying to live according to its disciplines.

When he was 20, Stephen married Gisela, the sister of the duke of Bavaria, the future Emperor Henry II — another married saint whom we will consider in the next chapter. Two years later, in 997, Stephen succeeded his father as head of the Magyars, with the title of duke.

Hungary was then at peace with its neighbors and Stephen devoted himself to rooting out idolatry among his people. He went in disguise with Christian missionaries and sometimes had to keep those missionaries from imposing Christianity forcibly.

Alas, peace was not to last. Some German Christian knights had immigrated into the fertile plains of Hungary and they were taking land that the Magyars thought was theirs. The peasants revolted under the leadership of Koppany. Stephen took the side of the German Christians. He prepared himself for battle by fasting, almsgiving and prayer, invoking the intercession of St. Martin of Tours. The battle took place in 998 at Veszprem and, although badly outnumbered, Stephen's forces won a victory. Koppany was slain.

In thanksgiving for his victory, Stephen had a monastery dedicated to St. Martin built on the site of the battle. It came to be known as the Archabbey of Martinsberg, or Pannonhalma, and it flourished down to modern times. It became the motherhouse of all the Benedictine congregations in Hungary.

Stephen then invited many more missionaries to Hungary — from Germany, France and Italy. As they built churches and monasteries they also brought a semblance of civilization to the barbarian country. Stephen even founded dioceses: the Archdiocese of Gran with five suffragan dioceses and, later, the Archdiocese of Kalocsa, with three suffragan dioceses.

Having founded the dioceses, Stephen sent Abbot Astrik, whom he designated to be the first archbishop, to Rome to obtain Pope Silvester II's approval for these foundations and for a proper ecclesiastical organization. He also had Abbot Astrik ask the pope to confer on Stephen the title of king. As it happened, the duke of Poland, Boleslaus, had also sent an embassy to Rome to get the title of king, and Pope Silvester seemed inclined to grant the request. But, because of what Stephen was doing for the Church in Hungary, the pope decided that he should have priority.

The pope had prepared an elaborate crown for Boleslaus. The upper part of this crown, decorated with jewels and enameled figures of Christ and the apostles, was fitted on the lower part of a crown given to King Geza I by the Eastern Emperor Michael VII. The pope entrusted this crown to Abbot Astrik along with a papal bull that confirmed all the religious foundations Stephen had erected and the ordination of the Hungarian bishops of the new dioceses. Upon Abbot Astrik's return to Hungary, Stephen went out to meet him and listened with great reverence while the abbot read the papal bull.

The same Abbot Astrik, now Archbishop of Gran, crowned Stephen king with great solemnity on Christmas Day in the year 1001. St. Stephen's Crown was kept as a prized treasure of the Hungarian people until World War II, when it fell into the hands of Nazi Germany. After the war it was entrusted to the United States government, which kept it throughout the time that Hungary was governed by a communist government. After Hungary regained its independence, the United States returned the crown to the Hungarian government.

Once crowned king, Stephen spearheaded the continued growth of Christianity in his country. He ordered a majestic church in honor of Mary to be built at Stuhlweissenburg, where the kings of Hungary were afterwards crowned and buried. He founded the monastery of Sts. Peter and Paul in Buda and hospices for pilgrims in Rome, Ravenna and Constantinople. He founded four more monasteries for the Benedictines to complement the one he had founded at Martinsberg. He established convents for nuns. One result of all this building was that the road commonly used by European pilgrims going to the Holy Land was made safer.

To support all this building, Stephen commanded that a system of tithes be set up. He also required that at least one out of every 10 towns had to build a church and support a priest. Stephen himself furnished the churches out of the royal treasury.

He went on to pass edicts for the severe punishment of blasphemy, murder, theft and adultery. He commanded all of his subjects to marry except monks, nuns and clergy, but he forbade marriages between Christians and pagans.

Stephen was known for his virtue and for his willingness to help the poor in his kingdom. He listened to their complaints and he took widows and orphans under his special protection. He even disguised himself in order to travel among his people to find out the needs that his officials might overlook. During one of these sojourns he was attacked by a band of beggars, who knocked him down and stole his purse. When the king's officials heard of it, they insisted that he should not expose himself to such danger again. Stephen simply renewed his vow never to refuse alms to anyone who begged of him.

Besides furthering the expansion of Christianity in his domain, Stephen undertook the complete reorganization of Hungary's political system. He abolished old tribal divisions and partitioned the country into counties, using a system of governors similar to that of Western European countries. He also developed a form of feudalism, turning independent nobles into vassals of the crown. He retained tight control over the common people to prevent undue accumulation of power into the hands of the nobles. He was the architect of the independent realm of Hungary.

All these reforms didn't please everybody. In 1025 there was a revolt led by a noble named Ajton. Stephen mobilized his forces and won a victory at Kalocsa.

But Stephen didn't like wars and did everything he could to prevent them. When, in 1024, his saintly brother-in-law, Emperor Henry II, died, he was succeeded by his cousin, Conrad II. Conrad considered Stephen's growing power to be a threat so he led troops against Hungary. Instead of fighting, Stephen arranged for a parley with Conrad and a peaceful settlement was arranged.

While Stephen was ruling Hungary and furthering the expansion of Christianity, he was also being a good father. He and Gisela had one son, Emeric, whom they reared to emulate his father. As the years passed, Stephen began to entrust parts of his government to his son. Then tragedy occurred: Emeric was killed in a hunting accident in 1031. The Catholic Church was later to declared Emeric blessed.

With the death of his son, Stephen was left without an heir and the last years of his life were embittered by family disputes about the succession. Eventually his nephew Peter succeeded him, but before his death Stephen was the target of an assassination attempt by two of his cousins. A hired killer managed to enter Stephen's bedroom while he was suffering from a painful illness. The king awoke, saw that the man planned to kill him, and calmly called out, "If God be with me, who shall be against me?" The man begged forgiveness, which Stephen readily granted.

Stephen died at age 63 on the feast of the Assumption in 1038. He was buried beside his son Emeric at Stuhlweissenburg and his shrine there soon became the scene of miracles. Forty-five years later, King Ladislaus ordered his relics enshrined in the church of Our Lady at Buda.

Stephen was canonized in 1083. His feast is celebrated on August 16, the day after the feast of the Assumption.

ST. HENRY

Although St. Henry is one of the married saints in the Church's liturgical calendar, the fact that he was married was only incidental to his being canonized. Indeed, we don't know anything about his married life.

Henry was one of the German kings who held the title of emperor. The 11th century saw a number of Emperor Henrys, but the only one canonized was Emperor Henry II, born in Bavaria in 972. He was a typical king of his time, never hesitating to join in battle to protect his frontiers or to crush rebellions. Certainly, from a 20th century standpoint, he was too quick to fight wars, but he should be judged according to the standpoint of the moral standards of his own time.

Henry is known for cooperating with Benedictine abbeys in the restoration of ecclesiastical and social discipline. Like his brother-in-law, St. Stephen, he was concerned about furthering Christianity.

Henry II's life was closely entwined with that

of Pope Benedict VIII, pope from 1012 to 1024. But to understand how the lives of these two men came to be connected, we must start with the situation of the papacy at the beginning of the 11th century. At that time, it was under the control of the Crescentian family of Rome. Popes John XVII, John XVIII and Sergius were all elected by this family.

In 1012, though, when Pope Sergius died on May 12 and the leader of the Crescentian family, John II Crescentius, died six days later, a violent political upheaval took place in Rome and the Tusculan family was able to oust the Crescentii. The Tusculans chose and installed a layman as pope — Theophylact, the son of Count Gregory of Tusculum. While Theophylact took over the papacy his brother Romanus became civil ruler of Rome. A new Roman family now was in power. Theophylact assumed the name of Pope Benedict VIII.

The Crescentii, however, weren't willing to give up the papacy, so they elected one of their own, a man named Gregory. With the Tusculans in power, though, Gregory could not gain access to the Lateran Palace, the home of the popes. So Gregory made his way to Germany to appeal to King Henry II. Henry received Gregory and promised to settle the dispute when he had time to go to Rome. Meanwhile, Henry took Gregory's ceremonial cross from him and told him not to exercise his office.

However, Henry had apparently already realized that the Tusculans, and Benedict VIII, were in full control of the papacy. Henry recognized Benedict as the rightful pope and Gregory, now considered an antipope, disappeared from history.

After Henry declared Benedict to be the rightful pope, Benedict crowned Henry emperor in St. Peter's Basilica in February 1014.

After Henry's coronation, the pope and the emperor went to Ravenna where they held a synod that had the expressed purpose of reforming the Church. Through the years many abuses had crept into the Church, thanks to the poor quality of some of the popes at that time. In some places the episcopacy had become a hereditary caste and it was common for priests to have children. The preaching of sermons was largely discontinued, sacraments were neglected, and the faith of the people was corrupted by superstition.

The synod at Ravenna legislated against the simony that was prevalent, and also settled the minimum age for Holy Orders.

Henry then returned to Germany and Benedict, for the next six years, tried to make the papal states stronger politically and militarily. He himself took part in a sea battle against Arab invaders in northern Italy and liberated Sardinia in 1016. In the south he supported revolts against the Byzantines who ruled there. He restored papal authority in the Campagna and formed alliances with Pisa and Genoa.

In 1019, though, the Byzantines defeated those who revolted in southern Italy and started moving north. This time Benedict thought he had better seek Henry's help, so he traveled to Germany. His appearance on German soil created a great impression on the German people.

Henry agreed to help Benedict against the Byzantines and in 1022 the emperor and the pope led a powerful army to southern Italy. The Byzantine threat was stopped, at least temporarily. Naturally, these battles against the Byzantines did not endear Benedict to the Church of Constantinople. The pope's name was removed from the diptychs, the tablets that contained the names of those prayed for during the canon of the liturgy in the Church of the East.

Now that Emperor Henry and Pope Benedict were together again in Italy, they cooperated some more in attempting reforms of the Church. At a synod in Pavia in 1022 they passed legislation that prohibited marriage and concubinage for all clerics and reduced the children of such unions to serfdom. It was Henry who took the lead in this reform, for religious reasons. For Benedict's part, as his address at the synod made clear, his main concern was that Church property was too often dissipated when the clergy married and had families.

Both Pope Benedict VIII and King Henry II died in 1024, the pope having served in the papacy for 12 years and Henry having been king in Germany for 20 years and emperor for 10. Benedict was succeeded by his brother Romanus, who had been civil ruler of Rome. There was scandal involved because Romanus was said to have obtained the papacy through bribery and because Romanus was elevated from layman to pope in a single day. He took the name Pope John XIX.

Henry II was succeeded by Conrad II, who was considerably different from his predecessor. Unlike Henry who worked cooperatively with Benedict, Conrad regarded the pope as of little consequence and a man he could use.

Henry was canonized in 1146. His feast day is celebrated on July 13.

ST. MARGARET OF SCOTLAND

S t. Margaret is among the most famous and important of all people, men and women, in the history of Scotland. The things she did during her relatively short life — she died when she was 46 — influenced Scotland's future. But above all, she was a holy woman, a loyal and wise partner to her husband, and a model Christian mother to her eight children.

However, the most famous queen in Scotland's history wasn't Scottish by birth. On her father's side, she was English, or, more accurately, Saxon. On her mother's side, she was Bavarian. But she wasn't born and reared either in England or in Bavaria, but in Hungary. Furthermore, this Hungarian-born, English-Bavarian queen of Scotland owed much to two other married saints, St. Stephen of Hungary and St. Edward the Confessor, for her fervent faith.

Obviously, we must review a bit of history to unravel all that.

During the 9th century, England was overwhelmed by the Vikings of Denmark. Only the kingdom of Wessex, in southern England, was able to hold out against the Danes. There King Alfred the Great was able to drive the Danes from part of the land they had conquered, preserving the Saxon influence there. However, early in the 11th century, the Danes, led by Canute the Great, invaded again. Canute was to rule as king of England from 1016 to 1035.

With the Dane Canute in complete control of England, the Saxon heirs to Alfred the Great's throne had to get out of England. One of those heirs was Edward the Confessor, who fled to Normandy where he lived from 1013 to 1040. His nephews, Edmund and Edward, found refuge in Hungary, where they were befriended by St. Stephen, king of Hungary. Edward d'Outremer (The Exile) married Agatha, the niece of St. Stephen's wife Gisela and a relative of another married saint, Emperor Henry II. Edward and Agatha had three children — Margaret; Christina, who later was to become the abbess of a monastery in Romsey, Hampshire; and Edgar, known as "the Aetheling," Saxon for "the Prince." All three children were educated in secular subjects and in Christian virtues in the court of St. Stephen along with his son, Emeric.

In 1035, England's Danish King Canute died and was succeeded by his two sons, both of whom died within a short time without heirs. Therefore,

in 1040, Edward the Confessor was invited back
to England and he was crowned king in 1042. Since
he had no son of his own, he offered to make his
nephew, Edward the Exile (Margaret's father), his
successor. So in 1057, when Margaret was 10, her
family left Hungary for England.

Shortly after they reached England, though,
Margaret's father died suddenly. This left her
brother, Edgar the Aetheling, next in line for the
throne. So Edward the Confessor took Agatha and
her children into his court. During the nine years
Margaret lived in St. Edward's court, she could
hardly not have been affected by the example
which her saintly granduncle gave in his piety and
generosity to the Church and the poor.

When St. Edward the Confessor died in 1066,
the leaders of England's nobility decided that Edgar
the Aetheling was too young to assume the crown.
Instead, they offered it to Harold, the son of
Godwin, Earl of Wessex and brother of St.
Edward's wife Edith. As Harold was accepting the
kingship the Danes used the opportunity to invade
England again and Harold went with his fleet to
the north of England to put down the invasion.
Then Duke William of Normandy took advantage
of that opening to cross the English Channel to
claim the crown for himself. Harold's fleet returned
south in a weakened condition and William defeated him in the famous battle of Hastings on
October 14, 1066. Harold was killed in the battle

and William the Conqueror controlled England.

With this turn of events, Agatha decided it was time for her to get her family out of England. First they went to Northumbria in northern England. Then they put out to sea, probably intending to return to Hungary. However, a violent storm drove the ship to the shores of Scotland. They found shelter from the storm in a little bay on the north shore of the Firth of Forth, still known today as "St. Margaret's Hope." They were about five miles from the Tower of Dunfermline, where Malcolm III reigned as king of Scotland. Malcolm gave the refugees a warm welcome and they remained in Scotland.

Malcolm was the son of King Duncan I, who had been murdered by Macbeth (later memorialized by William Shakespeare). After his father's death, Malcolm had escaped to England where he took refuge in St. Edward the Confessor's court. He might have met Margaret there. Later, he managed to return to Scotland and defeat Macbeth in 1054. He was crowned king in 1057 at Scone.

The ancient English chroniclers called Malcolm savage and ruthless, but St. Aelred of Rievaulx, his contemporary, said of him: "He was a king very humble in heart, bold in spirit, exceedingly strong in bodily strength, daring though not rash, and endowed with many other good qualities." He was apparently not a ruthless savage, but still, to Agatha and her family, not exactly the sort of man who would have met the high standards of the court of England.

Margaret was in her early 20's by this time, a beautiful, charming, intelligent and cultured young woman. It's hardly a surprise, therefore, that Malcolm was attracted to her and soon asked her to marry him. He was already a widower, his first wife, Ingibiorg, having given him a son, Prince Duncan. Margaret seems to have had desires to enter the convent, as her sister Christina did, but she apparently recognized the will of God in directing the course of her life so that she could do much good for the people of Scotland.

Therefore, in 1070, Malcolm and Margaret were married in the little chapel of Dunfermline Tower by Fothad, Bishop of St. Andrews. Margaret was 23, Malcolm about 40. Their union proved to be a remarkably happy one, lasting until their deaths 23 years later.

The principal source of information about St. Margaret is Turgot, a monk who was her confessor. (Later he became the Bishop of St. Andrews.) In his biography, he said that Margaret had a character that was both strong and gentle. He says that she knew how to bring her husband to her way of thinking even while she let him believe that they were largely his own ideas which he put into practice. Turgot said that all the great things Margaret accomplished rose from her ardent love of God and for the Catholic Church. He said: "The prudent queen directed all such things as it was fitting for her to regulate: the laws of the realm were administered by her counsel; by her care the influence of religion was extended, and the people rejoiced in the prosperity of her affairs."

While she was helping her husband conduct affairs of state, Margaret never forgot that her first responsibility was to her children. She and Malcolm had six boys — Edward, Edmund, Edgar, Aethelred, Alexander, and David, and two girls — Matilda (also called Maud) and Mary. She personally disciplined the children carefully and they grew up well-behaved and instructed in their religion as well as in all the branches of learning at that time.

Just as St. Stephen had done in Hungary, Margaret made it her constant effort to obtain good priests and teachers for all parts of Scotland. She formed a guild of women to embroider vestments for priests. She and Malcolm founded several churches, notably that of the Holy Trinity at Dunfermline, and she rebuilt the churches that had been erected at the time of the glorious Celtic Church but devastated during the Viking invasions. Among these churches was the one on the island of Iona from which St. Columba and his Irish monks had originally brought the faith to Scotland. Another was the one at St. Andrews. She furnished these churches with splendid ornaments, chalices and other sacred vessels of pure gold.

She also gathered an extensive library, first at Dunfermline and later at Edinburgh, of valuable manuscripts, especially of the Scriptures. And she brought to her court learned clerics for discussions on various topics of the day. These discussions probably were held in Latin, but it is interesting to note that it was under King Malcolm and Queen Margaret that English replaced Gaelic as the regular language of the Scottish court. This was undoubtedly because Margaret did not speak Gaelic very well.

Margaret is also known for her efforts to reform the Church in Scotland. This was a time when the Universal Church was badly in need of reform and this was being done in Rome by popes such as the great St. Gregory VII. Margaret tried to follow his lead and, to do so, she sought the counsel of such men as Lanfranc, the Italian scholar who became Archbishop of Canterbury and was one of the foremost restorers of the Church in France and England. Archbishop Lanfranc sent clerics to Scotland to help Margaret.

The Church in Scotland badly needed reforming, mainly because it had been cut off from the rest of Christendom by the Viking invasions. Besides the churches that were in ruins, Margaret found ancient customs and rites still in use. To bring Scotland's Church up to date with the rest of the Church, and to try to correct religious abuses such as simony, usury and incestuous marriages,

Margaret instigated councils and synods. Turgot wrote about one of those councils that lasted three days. Margaret urged the assembled ecclesiastics to discard their local customs and conform to the practices of the Holy Roman Church. She addressed the men in English, but then Malcolm repeated what she had said in Gaelic to make sure the clerics understood.

Margaret was less than 100 percent successful, however, in her attempt to do away with the holding of ecclesiastical benefices by laymen. This custom had become too ingrained in the Scottish Church. However, very gradually during her reign and that of her sons there evolved a Catholic Church that was truly spiritual and that had thrown off the moral decay that was present when she arrived in Scotland.

The main reason Margaret was able to accomplish this was because of her evident personal sanctity. Turgot wrote: "Of all living persons I know or have known, she was the most devoted to prayer and fasting, to works of mercy and almsgiving." She had certain times for prayer and for reading Scripture. She ate sparingly and slept little in order to have time for her devotions. At night she often rose at midnight and went to the Abbey Church at Dunfermline for the Divine Office. She attended Mass in the morning and on festivals sometimes assisted at as many as five or six Masses. In Dunfermline there is a grotto, still called St.

Margaret's Cave, where she often went alone at night to spend hours in contemplation and prayer.

Malcolm's obvious love for his wife is reflected in the influence she had over the spiritual life of this Scottish warrior. Unlike other husbands of saints included in this book, who merely tolerated their wives' spirituality, Malcolm not only allowed his wife to practice her devotions, he often joined her. They kept two Lents, one at the usual time before Easter and another before Christmas.

Margaret was also known for her charity. It is said that, on her way home from the abbey church, she would wash the feet of six poor persons and give them alms. She even taught Malcolm to do this and his biographer says, "It must have astounded the court to see the king kneel to wash the feet of the poor whom his wife devotedly attended every day. He also helped her wait on them at table as she fed them." It is recorded that she never sat down to eat without first feeding nine orphans and 24 adults, although no one seems to know why those particular numbers were significant.

She never refused the beggars who flocked to her. Often her gifts outran her means, but those around her vied with each other to offer her their own belongings to aid her charity. She was even known to pilfer things from the king who, when he caught her with his money in his hands, would laugh and say that he would have her arrested.

St. Andrews was a place of pilgrimage for those who wanted to visit the place where, it was believed, the relics of St. Andrew the Apostle were. St. Andrews was on the north side of the Firth of Forth and Dunfermline on the south side. So Margaret erected hostels at St. Andrews and inaugurated a free ferry service across the Firth of Forth. This ferry service (no longer free) remained the only way to cross the Firth until the end of the 19th century, when a bridge was built. Towns on each side of the Firth are still known as North Queensferry and South Queensferry, both named after Margaret.

Another place named after Margaret is "Margaret's Stone." A large stone shaped like a seat on the North Queensferry road near Dunfermline, it is believed to have been one of Margaret's judgment seats. She sat there while holding open court, in order to be accessible to all the people.

The end of Margaret's life proved to be tragic. She became ill and lay for six months in Edinburgh Castle, wracked with pain. Then the English king, William Rufus, son of William the Conqueror, violated the treaty his father had made with Malcolm and seized several Scottish castles in Northumberland. Malcolm and two of his sons, Edward and Edgar, led troops to recover the castle at Alnwick, but Malcolm and Edward were killed in the battle.

Back in Edinburgh, Margaret had a premonition of this result. On November 16, 1093, three days after the battle took place, but before word got back to Edinburgh, she seemed to rally from her illness. She went to her little chapel in the castle where she heard Mass and received Viaticum. She then returned to her bed, where her sickness became even worse and it was clear that death was imminent. She asked the clergy to recite the prayers for the dying and she asked that the Black Rood, a richly ornamented cross of pure gold containing a relic of the True Cross, be brought to her. Holding this relic, she quietly recited Psalm 51, the *Miserere*.

At that moment her son Edgar entered the room. He had just returned from the scene of battle where his father and brother had been killed. When Margaret asked about her husband and son, Edgar hesitated. But Margaret said, "I know it, my boy, I know it. By this Holy Cross, by the bond of our blood, I adjure you to tell me the truth." When Edgar told her what had happened, she accepted the news with resignation. Then she began to recite the prayer she always said before receiving Communion: "Lord Jesus Christ, who according to the will of the Father, through the cooperation of the Holy Ghost, hast by Thy death given life to the world, deliver me..." — and died.

Margaret was buried in the Abbey Church in Dunfermline. Pilgrimages to her burial place began shortly after her death as the Scottish people venerated her as a saint. However, she wasn't canonized until 156 years later, on August 5, 1249, by Pope Innocent IV. After that a new and more elaborate tomb was built in the Abbey Church at Dunfermline and she was reburied there, next to her husband, King Malcolm.

Margaret's body remained there for three centuries as vigil lights burned night and day. But in the 16th century, when John Knox was protesting the Catholic religion, the monks at Dunfermline prudently removed Margaret's relics and took them to a more secure place. When Knox's fanatics stormed the Abbey Church they destroyed the shrine, leaving only the marble base on which St. Margaret's tomb had stood, but they did not find the relics.

For a while, St. Margaret's head was kept by Mary, Queen of Scots, at Edinburgh Castle. Later it was taken to the Catholic College of Douai, France, from which it disappeared during the French Revolution. The rest of her relics were received by Philip II of Spain who placed them in the Escorial Palace in Madrid.

St. Margaret was named patroness of Scotland in 1673.

Margaret's seven surviving children reflected the care with which they had been reared. Three of the sons — Edgar, Alexander and David — were each in turn kings of Scotland. Aethelred became Abbot of Dunkeld. Only Margaret and Malcolm's second son, Edmund, turned out to be the "black sheep" in the family. Apparently under the influence of Malcolm's brother Donald Bane, who wanted the crown for himself, Edmund proved treacherous and disloyal and was stripped of his royal rank and right of succession. However, in later years he repented and died a monk in the monastery of Montecute in Somersetshire.

Margaret and Malcolm's daughters were both educated in the convent of their aunt, Christina, and later entered into illustrious marriages. Matilda married King Henry I of England and was known by the English as "good Queen Maud." Mary married Count Eustace III of Boulogne. Her daughter Matilda, Margaret's granddaughter, became the wife of King Stephen of England, the successor of Henry I.

In Scotland, the descendants of Malcolm and Margaret ruled for 200 years, a period considered to have been Scotland's golden era. Their son David was particularly considered a great king and a holy person. After his death he was venerated in Scotland as a saint. He continued his mother's work, rendering great service to the Church. An old poem about him showed his mother's lasting influence:

> The day he was both king and knight;
> a monk devout he was by night.

ST. EDWARD THE CONFESSOR

S t. Edward the Confessor is not in the Church's liturgical calendar, but he does have a feast day assigned to him — October 13. This brief profile is included because he is a married saint and because he had an influence on St. Margaret of Scotland.

The history of England around the time that Edward lived is recounted in the chapter about St. Margaret of Scotland.

Edward was born in 1003 in England, the son of Ethelred the Redeless by his Norman wife Emma. When the Danish King Canute conquered England, Edward fled to the continent in 1013 and lived at Normandy. He remained there, soaking up French culture until he was invited back to England in 1042. He was king of England for almost 22 years, until his death in 1066.

Edward married Edith, the daughter of Godwin, in 1044. It has traditionally been claimed that, as an aspect of his sanctity — for the love of God and greater perfection — he and Edith lived in absolute continence, as brother and sister. If true, this fact might indicate an imperfect understanding of the teachings of the Church regarding the role and purpose of sexual relations in marriage. It might also indicate that Edward was not attracted sexually to women.

Whether he and Edith lived as brother and sister or not, the fact is that they had no children. Therefore, the succession to the throne was always an open question. It was the reason why St. Margaret of Scotland's father, Edward d'Outremer, returned with his family from exile in Hungary, expecting to become England's next king. However, he died shortly after his return to England.

Since Edward had lived most of his life in France, the English court was more Norman-French in culture and politics than it was English. The Norman influence was felt in the appointment of bishops and other offices. The chief opponent of the Norman influence was Edward's father-in-law, Godwin. After a series of incidents, a crisis developed and Godwin and his family were banished. Even Edward's wife Edith was confined to a convent for a time (which would be reason enough not to consider Edward as a model husband). Eventually, though, Godwin was permitted to return and an agreement was made that Frenchmen would no longer be appointed to bishoprics. The Norman Archbishop of Canterbury and another bishop fled across the English Channel.

If Edward didn't seem a model husband, he was a saintly man in other aspects. He was known for his just administration and for being generous to the poor and strangers. He attended Mass every day, even when he was away from the court for days at a time enjoying his favorite diversion, hunting. He made a commanding appearance since he was tall and well-built, with a ruddy face and white hair and beard.

While he was in exile in Normandy, Edward had made a vow to go on pilgrimage to St. Peter's Tomb in Rome if God saw fit to reverse the misfortune his family was then experiencing. After he was crowned as king of England, he announced this vow to his council and his desire to fulfill it. Council members, though, advised against his leaving the country because it would be exposed to domestic divisions and to foreign enemies. Edward decided that the matter should be referred to the pope, Leo IX.

Pope Leo acknowledged the impracticality of Edward's leaving England. Therefore, he dispensed him from his vow upon the condition that he should give to the poor the sum of money that he would have spent on his journey to Rome, and that he should build or repair, and endow, a monastery in honor of St. Peter. Accordingly, King Edward rebuilt and endowed an abbey already existing in a place close to London. Because of its location, it was called Westminster Abbey.

A new choir for the Abbey Church was consecrated with great solemnity on the feast of the Holy Innocents in 1065. However, King Edward was too ill to attend the ceremony. He died a week later, on January 5, 1066 and was buried in the abbey. He was canonized in 1161.

St. Edward the Confessor is a popular saint in the Church of England, the Anglicans, and Episcopalian churches in the United States are frequently named after him. Of course, he lived 500 years before the Protestant Reformation.

ST. BRIDGET OF SWEDEN

S t. Bridget of Sweden is known primarily for her extraordinary visions and for the revelations she received during those visions. She is also recognized for founding a religious order, the Brigittines. As is true of our other married saints, the fact that she was married seems to have been incidental. She was not only married, she was the mother of eight children.

There are two St. Bridgets on the Church's liturgical calendar, and neither has the spelling right. The great fifth- and sixth-century Irish abbess, who of course was not married, should be called St. Brigid. And Bridget of Sweden was known as Birgitta during her lifetime.

That lifetime began about the year 1303, at Finstad near Uppsala. Her father was Birger Persson, the governor of Upland, the most important province in Sweden. He was one of the wealthiest landowners in the country. Bridget's mother was Ingeborg Bengtsdotter, Birger's second wife. Both Birger and Ingeborg were devout

Christians and saw to it that their children received a good Christian education.

Although there doesn't seem to have been anything unusual about the way Bridget was reared, she began to have visions as early as the age of seven. They were to continue for the rest of her life.

Bridget's mother died when she was 12 and for the next year or so she was reared by an aunt at Aspenas on Lake Sommen. But when she was only 13 she was married to the 18-year-old Ulf Gudmarsson, the Prince of Nierck. Their marriage was a very happy one, blessed, as already mentioned, with eight children — four boys and four girls. One of them, her youngest daughter, was later canonized as St. Catherine of Sweden.

The family lived on a feudal estate at Ulfasa and Bridget's reputation for charity and piety began to grow. She founded a hospital and took a personal interest in caring for the sick there. Bridget and Ulf also cultivated the friendship of the most learned and pious theologians in Sweden. One of them, Blessed Nicholas Hermansson, Bishop of Linkoping, became her children's tutor.

Bridget and Ulf had been married for 19 years in 1335 when they were summoned to serve in the court of the young king of Sweden, Magnus II. Bridget became the principal lady-in-waiting for Queen Blanche. Both the king and queen lived frivolous lives and enjoyed the luxuries available to them; in fact, King Magnus was described as wicked. Bridget did everything she could to influence the queen for good, but her efforts were not always taken seriously. As her personal revelations and visions continued, Bridget found herself the butt of court gossip. "What was the Lady Bridget dreaming about last night?" became a common question.

Meanwhile, Bridget and Ulf began to have problems with their children. Their eldest daughter had married a riotous noble and was having marital problems. Then their youngest son, Gudmar, died in 1340. In their grief, Bridget and Ulf made a retreat at the shrine of St. Olaf of Norway at Trondhjem.

After their pilgrimage, they returned to the Swedish court and again tried to influence King Magnus and Queen Blanche. Meeting with no more success than before, they asked permission to go on pilgrimage to the shrine of St. James at Compostela, Spain, then the most popular shrine in all of Europe. They received permission and their journey lasted from 1341 to 1343.

As they were returning from Compostela, Ulf became dangerously sick at Arras in northern France. It appeared that he was about to die and Bridget implored heaven with her prayers for his recovery. Ulf himself vowed that if he recovered he would enter a monastery when they got back to Sweden. In a vision, St. Denis assured Bridget that Ulf would recover and make it back to Sweden. He did recover and he kept his vow: He entered the Cistercian monastery at Afvastra. He died there in 1344, shortly after he had finished his novitiate and taken his religious vows.

When Ulf entered the monastery, Bridget took up residence nearby and began a life of prayer and penance. Her austerities became so great that her confessor had to warn her to be more moderate. Then her visions and revelations began to become more insistent, so much so that she became alarmed that she was being deluded by the devil or by her own imagination. In answer to her doubts, she received the same vision three times, each time telling her to submit her visions to Master Matthias, a priest with great experience and learning. Bridget did so, and he pronounced them to be from God.

From then on, Bridget communicated her visions to Father Peter Olavsson, the prior of the Cistercian monastery, who wrote them down. Therefore, the Church has a record of those revelations and examined them carefully during the canonization process. It determined that there was nothing in them that was contrary to faith and morals. (We'll say more about these revelations at the end of this chapter.)

As Bridget continued to have these visions, they culminated in a command from Christ to go to the royal court and warn King Magnus that God was going to judge him harshly for his sins. Like a prophet from the Old Testament, she went to the court and denounced the king, the queen, the nobles and the bishops. Perhaps surprisingly, this time they actually had some effect. King Magnus mended his ways, at least for a while. He also provided the land and an endowment for a new type of monastery that Bridget, in response to another vision, planned to found at Vadstena.

This monastery in Bridget's vision was to be primarily for women, but it was also to have a special wing for monks. The monks were to be responsible for the spiritual care of the nuns, but a mother abbess was responsible for the temporal affairs of the monks as well as the nuns. There were to be 60 nuns, 13 priests (in honor of the 12 apostles plus St. Paul), four deacons (in honor of the Doctors of the Church, only four at the time; today there are 33), and eight lay brothers. This brought the total number of men and women in the monastery to 85, the number of the 72 disciples of Christ plus the 12 apostles and St. Paul.

The men and women were kept strictly separated except while the monks were providing religious services for the nuns. In the church, the nuns' choir was above in a gallery, so that the men and women could not even see one another.

Bridget opened her first monastery in 1346, two years after Ulf's death. The Order spread throughout most of Europe, but most of the

Brigittine monasteries were destroyed during the religious troubles associated with the Protestant Reformation. However, the Order continues to exist. Today there are separate Religious Orders for men and women, the Brigittine Monks (with U.S. headquarters in Amity, Oregon) and the Brigittine Sisters (with U.S. headquarters in Darien, Connecticut). Their formal name is Order of the Most Holy Savior.

During Bridget's life, popes lived in Avignon, France rather than in Rome. In several of her visions, Bridget was ordered by Christ to appeal to the pope to return to Rome. She therefore wrote a letter to Pope Clement VI, urging him to return to Rome. When that got no response, she made up her mind to go personally to Avignon and to Rome. With that in mind, she left Sweden in the fall of 1349 along with her confessor, Father Peter Olavsson, and others. She wanted first to gain the indulgences associated with the Holy Year of 1350. She never returned to Sweden, spending most of the last 23 years of her life in Rome.

Her efforts to bring the papacy back to Rome were only partly successful. Working with others in Rome, she was able to convince Pope Urban V to return in 1367. He entered Rome with a strong military escort on October 16 of that year and moved into the Vatican. However, it wasn't a good time politically because there were revolts in Italy and in Rome itself. Eventually, Pope Urban had to seek refuge in Viterbo and then Montefiascone. He finally gave up and returned to Avignon in 1370.

It remained for another woman saint, Catherine of Siena, to convince another pope to return to Rome permanently. St. Catherine convinced Pope Gregory XI to take the papacy back to Italy to stay, but it was not accomplished until 1377. By then, Bridget had been dead for four years.

Even though Pope Urban had been unable to remain in Rome, Bridget's relations with him became strong enough that in 1370 he gave papal approbation to the Religious Order which she had founded.

Although she now made her residence in Rome, Bridget did a lot of traveling. During one of her visions, St. Francis of Assisi appeared to her and said, "Come, eat and drink with me in my cell." She took that as an invitation to go to Assisi, which she did, including the small cell St. Francis once used when he wanted to get away. Later, she made a tour of the other shrines in Italy, a trip that lasted for two years as she went from one to another.

Two churches in Rome are associated with St. Bridget. One is St. Paul's-Outside-the-Walls, which features a crucifix of Cavallini before which she prayed. The second is San Francesco a Ripa, where she experienced some visions.

Bridget was not alone in Rome. A few years

after she moved there, her daughter Catherine joined her and accompanied her on her travels.

Bridget's last pilgrimage was to the Holy Land, in 1373. This time she took with her not only Catherine but also her sons Charles and Birger, as well as a few other people. The trip did not go well. At Naples, while waiting for a ship, Charles got himself romantically involved with Queen Joanna I. Charles had a wife back in Sweden and Joanna's third husband was back in Spain. When she discovered what was happening, Bridget was horrified. Naturally, she prayed for an end to the affair. Whether as an answer to her prayer or just a natural occurrence, Charles suddenly became seriously ill. After suffering from the illness for two weeks, he died in his mother's arms. Two of Bridget's children had now preceded her in death.

After Charles' funeral, Bridget and her party continued to the Holy Land aboard ship. But there was a shipwreck off the coast of Palestine, near Jaffa, and Bridget almost drowned. Fortunately, she was rescued and finally was able to visit the places associated with Christ's life, death and resurrection. The pilgrimage, for Bridget, consisted of a series of intense visions of what had happened in those places.

Bridget and her party arrived back in Rome in March 1373. She had not been feeling well for some time and now her health began to decline seriously. On July 23, 1373, after receiving the last sacraments from her confessor, Father Peter, she died at the age of 70. She was buried in the Poor Clare Church of St. Lawrence, but four years later her body was carried across Europe back to Sweden, where it was placed in Bridget's first monastery of the Brigittine Order at Vadstena.

Bridget was canonized on October 7, 1391, only a little more than 18 years after her death, by Pope Boniface IX. Her feast is celebrated today on July 23. She is the patron saint of Sweden.

Since Bridget's visions were such an important part of her life, more should be said about them. Although the Church has stated that none of the revelations in her visions contained anything contrary to faith and morals, they are still "private revelations" and not part of the deposit of faith. Pope Benedict XIV referred to St. Bridget's revelations when he wrote: "Even though many of these revelations have been approved, we cannot and we ought not to give them the assent of divine faith, but only that of human faith, according to the dictates of prudence whenever these dictates enable us to decide that they are probable and worthy of pious credence."

Many of Bridget's revelations contain detailed information about the life of Christ and of Mary that are not contained in the New Testament. That's what made the revelations so popular in the Middle Ages. But are these any different from the thoughts any pious man or woman might summon from his or her imagination while meditating on the events in the life of Christ? That is for each person to decide for him or herself.

ST. ISIDORE AND
ST. MARIA DE LA CABEZA

In 1622, Pope Gregory XV canonized five saints: St. Ignatius of Loyola was the founder of the Society of Jesus (the Jesuits). St. Francis Xavier, one of the first Jesuits, was the great missionary to the Far East. St. Teresa of Avila was a great mystic, reformer of the Carmelites, and later declared a Doctor of the Church. St. Philip Neri was an Italian priest who founded the Congregation of the Oratory.

St. Isidore was a farmer and a married man.

In Spain, these four men and one woman are known as "the five saints." All except St. Philip Neri were from Spain. Today St. Isidore is the patron of Madrid, Spain, as well as of farmers.

He was born in Madrid in 1070 to parents so poor that his only inheritance was their plow. He was named after another St. Isidore, the renowned and learned seventh-century bishop of Seville, Spain. While still only a boy, barely old enough to wield a hoe, Isidore entered the service of John de Vergas, a wealthy resident of Madrid, as a farm worker on a large estate outside the city. Isidore lived and worked on that estate for the rest of his life.

He married a young woman known as Maria de la Cabeza, the daughter of other farmers just as poor as Isidore's parents. Isidore and Maria lived a holy life while fulfilling the vocations to which God had called them — a simple farmer and his wife. They had one child, a son, who died while he was still a child.

Isidore is known for nothing more than for leading a life of hard work, fervent prayer and lavish charity despite his poverty. He began each day with Mass in one of the city's churches and all day, as he walked behind his plow or performed other farm chores, he talked with God, his guardian angel or the saints. On public holidays he would visit the churches of Madrid and the neighboring districts. It was said of him, "In life his hand was ever on the plow, his heart ever blessed with the thought of God."

Isidore's practice of going to daily Mass aroused some resentfulness on the part of his fellow farm laborers because, they told John de Vergas, it made Isidore late for work. When confronted with this complaint, Isidore admitted that he was sometimes late for work, but, he said, "I do my utmost to make up for the few minutes snatched for prayer. And if you compare my work with that of the other plowers, you will find that I have not defrauded you."

This explanation didn't satisfy de Vergas so he decided to keep a close watch on Isidore. One morning he hid himself near a field where Isidore and other workers were working. Isidore was late, even later than usual, but started to plow the field, walking behind his plow and oxen. De Vergas began to get angry and was starting to leave his hiding place to confront Isidore when he stopped in astonishment. He could see plainly two angels, one on either side of Isidore and each with a plow, helping their companion make up the work lost while in prayer.

Isidore's generosity for the poor became well known. He frequently shared his simple meals with them, usually eating the scraps they left behind. One story recounts that Isidore had been invited to a dinner, but he was late as usual — absorbed in prayer in a church. When he arrived at the banquet he was followed by a troop of beggars. His hosts protested. They had saved enough food for him but they couldn't possibly feed the whole crowd. Isidore distributed the food to the beggars and there was plenty for everybody.

Isidore was also known for his love of animals. Again, there was a legend to illustrate that: On a snowy day one winter, he was carrying a sack of corn to be ground into cornmeal. He noticed a number of birds perched on the bare branches of a tree, unable to find any food on the snow-covered ground. He stopped, opened his sack, and, ignoring the jeers of a companion, poured out half of its contents for the birds. When Isidore and his companion arrived at their destination, the sack was still full. Furthermore, after it was ground, it produced double the usual amount of cornmeal.

St. Isidore died on May 15, 1130 at age 60. Maria died a few years later. The people of Madrid immediately honored both of them as saints and, some 40 years after his death, transferred his body to a more honorable shrine. There began to be reports of miracles after prayers for his intercession. In 1211 he is said to have appeared in a vision to King Alfonso of Castile, then fighting the Moors in the pass of Navas de Tolosa, and to have shown him an unknown path by means of which he was able to surprise and defeat the enemy.

St. Isidore's feast is celebrated on May 15. In 1995, the bishops of the United States approved the addition of St. Maria to the liturgical calendar. As this is being written, approval has not yet been given by the Vatican. In making its proposal to the U.S. bishops, the Bishops' Committee on the Liturgy noted, "Both Maria and Isidore are canonized saints. Although they were canonized at different times, they represent a husband and wife who were noted for holiness. Their commemoration provides the calendar with lay persons who are also a married couple, a category which is presently lacking in the calendar."

St. Isidore is the patron saint of the National Catholic Rural Life Conference. The conference composed a Litany of St. Isidore, as follows:

Lord, have mercy on us.
Christ, have mercy on us.
Lord, have mercy on us. Christ, hear us.
Christ, graciously hear us.
God, the Father of Heaven, have mercy on us.
God, the Son, Redeemer of the world...
God, the Holy Spirit...
Holy Trinity, one God...
Holy Mary, pray for us.
St. Isidore...
St. Isidore, patron of farmers...
St. Isidore, illustrious tiller of the soul...
St. Isidore, model of laborers...
St. Isidore, devoted to duty...
St. Isidore, loaded down with the labors of the field...
St. Isidore, model of filial piety...
St. Isidore, support of family life...
St. Isidore, confessor of the faith...
St. Isidore, example of mortification...
St. Isidore, assisted by angels...
St. Isidore, possessor of the gift of miracles...
St. Isidore, burning with lively faith...
St. Isidore, zealous in prayer...
St. Isidore, ardent lover of the Blessed Sacrament...

St. Isidore, lover of God's earth...
St. Isidore, lover of poverty...
St. Isidore, lover of humankind...
St. Isidore, most patient...
St. Isidore, most humble...
St. Isidore, most pure...
St. Isidore, most just...
St. Isidore, most obedient...
St. Isidore, most faithful...
St. Isidore, most grateful...
Jesus Our Lord, we beg of you, hear us.
That you would protect all tillers of the soil...
That you would bring to all a true knowledge of the stewardship of the land...
That you would preserve and increase our fields and flocks...
That you would give and preserve the fruits of the earth...
That you would bless our fields...
That you would preserve all rural pastors...
That you would grant harmony in our homes...
That you would lift up our hearts to you...
Be merciful, spare us, O Lord.
Be merciful, graciously hear us, O Lord.
From lightning and tempest, deliver us, O Lord.
From pestilence and flood...
From winds and drought...
From hail and storm...
From the scourge of insects...
From the spirit of selfishness...

Lamb of God, Who takes away the sins of the world, spare us, O Lord.

Lamb of God, Who takes away the sins of the world, graciously hear us, O Lord.

Lamb of God, Who takes away the sins of the world, have mercy on us.

Christ, hear us.

Christ, graciously hear us.

Let us pray. Grant, O Lord, that through the intercession of blessed Isidore the farmer, we may follow his example of patience and humility. May we walk faithfully in his footsteps that in the evening of life we may be able to present to you an abundant harvest of merit and good works, for you are the one God now and forever. Amen.

STS. PERPETUA AND FELICITY

S aints Perpetua and Felicity are among the
saints and martyrs included in the First Eu-
charistic Prayer — the Roman Canon — of
the Mass. Their memory has been preserved by
the Catholic Church from the time of their martyr
dom in the year 203. No saints were more univer-
sally honored in the early Church. This is partly
due to the fact that the account of their martyrdom is so precise and, one might say, even glam-
orized.

We know the details of Perpetua's and
Felicity's imprisonment because Perpetua kept a
careful diary during the time of her imprisonment.
The diary ends the day before she was killed with
the entry, "Of what was done in the games themselves, let him write who will." The diary was
finished by an eye-witness.

Vivia Perpetua was a noblewoman in the
North African city of Carthage, in modern Tunisia. She was the 22-year-old wife of a man in a
good position in the city and the mother of an

infant boy. She, her mother and two brothers were all Christians, but her father was a pagan.

Felicity was a slavewoman who accepted Christianity. When she was imprisoned she was an expectant mother. We don't know as much about her as we know about Perpetua and only what was in Perpetua's diary.

We hear frequently about the persecution of the early Church by the Romans. We shouldn't imagine, though, that this persecution was continuous. Rather it was sporadic. There were periods when the Christians were left in peace. The Roman emperors who were particularly ruthless in their persecution included Domitian around 95, Trajan from 107 to 112, Hadrian from 117 to 138, Marcus Aurelius from 161 to 180, Septimius Severus in 203, Decius from 249 to 251, Valerian in 257 and 258, and Diocletian in 303 and 304. Perpetua and Felicity died during the persecution of Septimius Severus, a Roman general whose bold military exploits led him to be proclaimed emperor after the death of Commodus, son of Marcus Aurelius.

Perpetua and Felicity were among a group of five Christians rounded up in Carthage on the orders of Septimius Severus. The others were two free men, Saturninus and Secundulus, and a slave, Revocatus. They were later joined by another man, Saturus, who was apparently their instructor in the faith and who chose to share their punishment. At first they were lodged in a private house under heavy guard, but later were moved to a prison.

Perpetua wrote in her diary that her father tried to save her life by urging her to renounce Christianity. "I said to my father, 'Do you see this vessel — water pot or whatever it may be? Can it be called by any other name than what it is?' 'No,' he replied. 'So also I cannot call myself by any other name than what I am — a Christian.' Then my father, provoked by the word 'Christian,' threw himself on me as if he would pluck out my eyes, but he only shook me, and in fact was vanquished.... Then I thanked God for the relief of being, for a few days, parted from my father."

During her imprisonment, Perpetua's greatest concern was for her baby. She wrote: "A few days later we were lodged in the prison, and I was much frightened, because I had never known such darkness. What a day of horror! Terrible heat, owing to the crowds! Rough treatment by the soldiers! To crown all I was tormented with anxiety for my baby. But Tertius and Pomponius, those blessed deacons who ministered to us, paid for us to be moved for a few hours to a better part of the prison and we obtained some relief."

Then, she said, her baby was brought to her and she nursed it, "for already he was faint for want of food." She wrote that she spoke to her mother about her baby and commended her son to her and to her brother. "For many days I suffered such anxieties," she wrote, "but I obtained leave for my child to remain in the prison with me, and when relieved of my trouble and distress for him, I quickly recovered my health. My prison suddenly became a palace to me and I would rather have been there than anywhere else."

By this time Perpetua and her fellow prisoners were determined that they would suffer death before they would renounce their faith. However, Perpetua's father didn't give up in his attempts to save her life. "Daughter," he said, "pity my white hairs! Pity your father, if I deserve you should call me father, if I have brought you up to this your prime of life, if I have loved you more than your brothers! Make me not a reproach to mankind! Look on your mother and your mother's sister, look on your son who cannot live after you are gone. Forget your pride; do not make us all wretched! None of us will ever speak freely again if calamity strikes you."

Perpetua's reaction to this exhortation was to feel pity for her father because, she wrote, "he alone of all my kindred would not have joy at my martyrdom." She thought that the Christians among her family would rejoice because she would be everlastingly happy in heaven.

The next day, her trial began at the forum in Carthage. The prisoners were placed on a platform. The judge was Hilarion, the procurator of the province. The others were questioned first and all confessed their faith.

When it was Perpetua's turn, her father suddenly appeared with her infant son. He implored Perpetua to "have pity on the child." Then Hilarion joined with her father and said, "Spare your father's white hairs. Spare the tender years of your child. Offer sacrifice for the prosperity of the emperor."

Perpetua replied, "No!"

Hilarion asked, "Are you a Christian?"

Perpetua replied, "Yes, I am."

At that her father ran up on the platform and tried to drag her down the steps, but Hilarion gave the order that he should be beaten off. With a rod, he was struck a blow. Perpetua said, "I felt as much as if I myself had been struck, so deeply did I grieve to see my father treated thus in his old age."

Hilarion then passed sentence, condemning them to the wild beasts. He had Saturus, Saturninus and Revocatus scourged (Secundulus seems to have died in prison before the trial), and Perpetua and Felicity beaten on the face. Hilarion then ordered that they be kept for the gladiatorial shows which were to be given for the soldiers on the festival of Geta, the young prince and the son of Severus. The prisoners returned to their cells, rejoicing.

Then, Perpetua wrote, "God so ordered it that my child no longer needed to nurse, nor did my milk incommode me."

Meanwhile, Felicity had feared that she might not be permitted to suffer for her faith as the others did because pregnant women were not sent to the arena. However, she gave birth in the prison to a daughter. One of their fellow Christians promptly adopted it.

The attitude of the prisoners resulted in many converts. One of them was their jailer, Pudens, who did everything he could for them. The day before the games, they were given the usual last meal, which the prisoners tried to make an *agape* meal. They sang psalms, prayed and spoke to those around them of the judgments of God and of their own joy in their sufferings.

On the day of their martyrdom, they marched from their cells to the amphitheater with cheerful looks and graceful bearing. The three men walked ahead and Perpetua and Felicity followed them, walking side by side, the noblewoman and the slave. At the gates of the amphitheater the attendants tried to force the men to put on the robes of the priests of Saturn and the women the dress symbolic of the goddess Ceres, but they all resisted and the officer allow them to enter the arena clad as they were.

As they entered the arena, Perpetua was singing. The three men called out warnings of the coming vengeance of God to the bystanders and to Hilarion, as they walked beneath his balcony.

Perhaps the rest of the story of their martyrdom can be told best from the Church's official story of their death. This is included in the Office of Readings, part of the Liturgy of the Hours, for March 7, their feast day:

"Perpetua was the first to be thrown down, and she fell prostrate. She got up and, seeing that Felicity was prostrate, went over and reached out her hand to her and lifted her up. Both stood up together. The hostility of the crowd was appeased, and they were ordered to the gate called Sanavivaria (where those not killed by the beasts were executed by gladiators). There Perpetua was welcomed by a catechumen called Rusticus. Rousing herself as if from sleep (so deeply had she been in spiritual ecstasy), she began to look around. To everyone's amazement, she said: 'When are we going to be led to the beasts?' When she heard that it had already happened she did not at first believe it until she saw the marks of violence on her body and her clothing.

"Then she beckoned to her brother and the catechumen, and addressed them in these words: 'Stand firm in faith, love one another and do not be tempted to do anything wrong because of our suffering.'

"Saturus, too, in another gate, encouraged the soldier Pudens, saying: 'Here I am, and just as I thought and foretold I have not yet felt any wild beast. Now believe with your whole heart: I will go there and be killed by the leopard in one bite.' And right at the end of the games, when he was thrown to the leopard he was in fact covered with so much blood from one bite that the people cried out to him, 'Washed and saved, washed and saved.'

And so, giving evidence of a second baptism, he was clearly saved who had been washed in this manner.

"Then Saturus said to the soldier Pudens: 'Farewell, and remember your faith as well as me; do not let these things frighten you; let them rather strengthen you.' At the same time he asked for the little ring from Pudens' finger. After soaking it in his wound he returned it to Pudens as a keepsake, leaving him a pledge and a remembrance of his blood. Half dead, he was thrown along with the others into the usual place of slaughter.

"The people, however, had demanded that the martyrs be led to the middle of the amphitheater. They wanted to see the sword thrust into the bodies of the victims, so that their eyes might share in the slaughter. Without being asked they went where the people wanted them to go; but first they kissed one another, to complete their witness with the customary kiss of peace.

"The others stood motionless and received the deathblow in silence, especially Saturus, who had gone up first and was first to die; he was helping Perpetua. But Perpetua, that she might experience the pain more deeply, rejoiced over her broken body and guided the shaking hand of the inexperienced gladiator to her throat. Such a woman — one before whom the unclean spirit trembled — could not perhaps have been killed, had she herself not willed it."

ST. PETER

Readers might think that the inclusion of St. Peter in this book about married saints is a bit unfair. After all, the fact that he was married is quite incidental, even unimportant. Besides, if we include St. Peter, why not include the other Apostles, most of whom probably were married?

Well, the premise of this book is simply that it's possible to be a saint whether one is married or unmarried. Most of those profiled in this book would have been saints whether or not they were married. They are all noted for something more than just being married. This is true of St. Peter, too.

And the reason none of the other Apostles are included is because Peter is the only one we know was married. We can conjecture that most of the others were married because most Jewish men, and women, were married. In fact, Judaism taught that it was a religious responsibility to marry and beget children. Only the Essenes among the Jews practiced celibacy. Nevertheless, we don't know which of the Apostles were married and which were not — except for St. Peter.

We know that Peter was married because the Gospels tell us that Jesus cured his mother-in-law: "Jesus entered the house of Peter, and saw his mother-in-law lying in bed with a fever. He touched her hand, the fever left her, and she rose and waited on him" (Matthew 8:14-15; see also Mark 1:29-31 and Luke 4:38-39).

Peter's original name was Simon. He and his brother Andrew were born in Bethsaida, on the northeastern shore of the Sea of Galilee. His father's name was Jonah. Jonah owned a prosperous fishing business, perhaps in partnership with Zebedee, the father of James and John. As Simon and Andrew grew up, they joined their father's business.

Simon married a woman from Capernaum, on the northern shore of the Sea of Galilee, a bit to the west of Bethsaida. He moved there and lived in a large housing complex called an *insula* — a cluster of rooms surrounded by alleys or hallways. An *insula* contained from 20 to 50 rooms for the several generations of families that usually lived there. Or unrelated families lived there in a sort of apartment house. The *insula* in which Peter and his family lived was a two-story structure with 42 rooms. We don't know if he built it or bought it, or if it was already owned by his in-laws. The ruins of this home are one of the most popular sites shown to tourists and pilgrims in the Holy Land.

Today a church is built over the ruins of Peter's home. Diagrams at the site show the layout of the structure, including the steps in several places that led from the first to the second story.

So Simon was living with his wife and mother-in-law in Capernaum and working in his father's fishing business. As a Jewish businessman he couldn't help but be influenced by some of the unrest in Galilee, where the Jews were ruled by the Romans. Simon lived near Gamla, where the Zealots movement was founded in the year 4 A.D. (of course, the years were not so designated at that time). The Zealots were so named because they were "zealous" for a return to the independence the Jews had had from the time of the Maccabees in 164 B.C. until the victory of King Herod the Great over the Hasmonaeans in 38 B.C. There had been several attempted revolts, all put down ruthlessly, but many of the Jews looked forward to the appearance of a messiah, someone who would lead a successful revolt against the Romans.

Then one day Simon's brother Andrew came up to him and said, "We have found the Messiah" (John 1:41). Andrew and another man had been listening to John the Baptist preach when a man named Jesus walked by. John said, "Behold, the Lamb of God." When Andrew and the other man heard that, they followed Jesus and ended up staying with him the rest of that day. He came away impressed, to say the least.

So Andrew took Simon to see Jesus. And "Jesus looked at him and said, 'You are Simon the son of Jonah; you will be called Kephas' (which is translated Peter)" (John 1:42). The word *kephas* is Aramaic for "the rock." The Greek equivalent is *petros*. Until Jesus renamed Simon it was unknown for Kephas to be used as a personal name.

Peter started to learn more about this man Jesus, but he continued to work as a fisherman. Later, though, after John the Baptist had been imprisoned by Herod Antipas, Jesus left his hometown of Nazareth to start preaching around the Sea of Galilee. One day he approached Simon Peter and Andrew while they were fishing and called to them, "Come after me, and I will make you fishers of men." They immediately followed him. Jesus then did the same with James and John, who had been fishing in a boat with their father Zebedee and some hired men. Simon's life was changed for good.

Jesus then moved into Peter's home in Capernaum. Soon people from all over were bringing the sick to the house to be cured. Jesus moved around to other villages where he preached, but returned to Peter's home in Capernaum. On one occasion, men who carried a paralytic to the home couldn't get in, so they climbed up to the roof, removed the roof covering and lowered the paralytic down to the room where Jesus was. (The Gospels don't record Peter's reaction.)

For a while, Peter's home was used by Jesus

as a sort of seminary for his apostles. They lived, ate, slept, studied and prayed there while Jesus tried to explain who he was and what his mission was. The apostles, though, Peter included, were slow to understand. Peter quickly became the leader of the apostles, his name always appearing at the top of the list of the apostles' names.

Then Herod Antipas executed John the Baptist and put out the word that he now wanted to "see" Jesus. Both John and Jesus attracted large crowds and it was easy for Antipas to imagine that those crowds could breed revolution. So Jesus, after praying on a mountain all night, decided it was time to spend less time in Galilee so as not to attract Herod Antipas' attention. Besides, he still wanted more time alone with the apostles to train them. So Peter left his family in Capernaum and started traveling with Jesus.

The first trip was to the Syrophoenician region of Tyre, in modern Lebanon along the Mediterranean Sea coast. From there they took a road that went east from Tyre to Damascus, Syria, but they didn't go all the way to Damascus. At Caesarea Philippi, the city in the Golan Heights built by Herod the Great's son Philip, they turned south and traveled to the eastern side of the Sea of Galilee. They then returned to Capernaum.

They weren't there long, though. Soon Jesus decided that they should go back to Caesarea Philippi and stay out of Galilee. He was safer in the territory ruled by Philip. Caesarea Philippi is at the base of Mount Hermon, a huge rock. While they were there, Jesus asked his apostles who people said that he was. They gave several replies. Then Jesus asked who the apostles said that he was. At that, Peter answered, "You are the Messiah, the Son of the Living God."

Jesus then said to him, "Blessed are you, Simon son of Jonah. For flesh and blood has not revealed this to you, but my heavenly Father. And so I say to you, you are Peter, and upon this rock I will build my church, and the gates of the netherworld shall not prevail against it. I will give you the keys to the kingdom of heaven. Whatever you bind on earth shall be bound in heaven; and whatever you loose on earth shall be loosed in heaven" (Matthew 16:16-19).

Six days later Jesus took Peter, along with James and John, up a high mountain where he was transfigured before them. Elijah and Moses appeared with Jesus. Peter was to remember that scene the rest of his life. He wrote about it in one of his letters, saying that he was an eyewitness of Christ's majesty: "For he received honor and glory from God the Father when that unique declaration came to him from the majestic glory, 'This is my Son, my beloved, with whom I am well pleased.' We ourselves heard this voice come from heaven while we were with him on the holy mountain" (2 Peter 1:17-18).

After the incident at Caesarea Philippi, Peter

appears frequently in the Gospels, not always favorably. He could not understand that Jesus wasn't going to be a political messiah and he protested when Jesus said that he, Jesus, was going to suffer and die. And then came that tragic night when Jesus' prophecy came true: Jesus was arrested. At first, Peter tried to protect Jesus, even drawing his sword and cutting off the ear of the high priest's servant. But Jesus told him to put away his sword and he healed the ear.

And then Peter's world fell apart. He followed those who had arrested Jesus to the courtyard of the high priest's home. When he was asked if he was one of Jesus' followers, he denied it three times. When Jesus was crucified, Peter was nowhere around. He recognized that he was not the heroic figure he thought himself to be. For the next few days he and the other apostles hid, afraid that those who had executed Jesus might come after them.

Then Peter received word from Mary of Magdala that Jesus' tomb was empty. He and John ran to the tomb and found that it was as Mary had said. Puzzled, they returned to the room where they had been staying and locked the doors. To their astonishment, that evening Jesus himself, risen from the dead, came into the room.

Jesus stayed with his apostles another 40 days before ascending into heaven. On one occasion, back in Galilee, Jesus again singled out Peter and made him declare three times that he loved him, paralleling the three times he had denied him. Each time Jesus told him, "Feed my sheep." He affirmed Peter's role as the leader of those who would follow Christ.

But Peter's character didn't really change until after Pentecost, when the Holy Spirit descended upon him and the other apostles. Suddenly they were no longer the fearful men who hid behind locked doors. Now they preached courageously and openly. When questioned by the Sanhedrin and ordered to stop preaching about Jesus, they refused to do it, even accepting imprisonment. Peter performed miracles similar to those that Jesus had performed: He cured a lame beggar and a paralyzed man named Aeneas, and he restored Tabitha back to life. Imprisoned twice, he was miraculously freed both times.

As there was more and more persecution in Jerusalem, Peter began to preach in the towns along the Mediterranean Sea, especially Lydda and Joppa. While he was in Joppa, he was asked to meet with a Gentile named Cornelius in the capital city of Caesarea. As he entered this huge city, it might well have been the first time he had ever been in a Gentile city because Jews at that time were careful to avoid Gentiles. Now, however, he came to realize that God wanted him to spread the message of Jesus to the Gentiles as well as to the Jews.

The first major controversy in the early Church concerned the conversion of Gentiles. Although Peter had accepted Cornelius as the first

Gentile convert, Paul and Barnabas were successful in converting thousands. Did those converts have to be circumcised first and observe the Jewish laws? Peter presided over the Council of Jerusalem that decided that they did not. The future of the new Church was to be among the Gentiles.

One of the cities where the Church was growing quickly was Antioch. Peter moved there and became bishop of that city. It was here that the followers of Jesus were first called Christians. We don't know how long he remained in Antioch, but eventually he moved on to Rome where he was considered to be the first bishop there. As such, he was also the Catholic Church's first pope.

We don't know how long he was in Rome, but a third-century legend claimed it was 25 years. This seems to be a deduction based on inconsistent chronological data. Ignatius of Antioch, who died in 107, said that Peter and Paul exercised joint authority over the Roman Church and Irenaeus, who died in 180, claimed that they jointly founded it and inaugurated its succession of bishops. Nothing is known, though, about the manner of their rule. In Rome's catacombs there are many wall writings that link the names of Peter and Paul, showing that devotion to them began in very early times.

We do know that Peter and Paul were both executed during the reign of Emperor Nero in either 64 or 67, probably the former. According to an old tradition, Peter was confined in the Mamertine prison in Rome, where the church of St. Peter in Chains now stands. Paintings show that his execution was by crucifixion and it is believed that he asked to be crucified upside down because he didn't feel worthy to be executed in the same manner as Jesus.

Peter was buried on Vatican Hill. Churches have been built over his tomb since the time of Constantine and the tomb is now under the main altar of St. Peter's Basilica.

But we aren't finished yet. In a book about married saints, we must ask the question, "What happened to Peter's wife?" Unfortunately, we have no satisfactory answer to that question. There is, however, every reason to believe that Peter's wife continued to go wherever Peter went. This surmise comes from Paul's First Letter to the Corinthians. In chapter nine, Paul defends himself against an apparent claim that he is not equal to the other apostles. Paul says, "My defense against those who would pass judgment on me is this. Do we not have the right to eat and drink? Do we not have the right to take along a Christian wife, as do the rest of the apostles, and the brothers of the Lord, and Kephas?" Apparently it was common knowledge that Peter traveled with his wife and Paul was saying that if Peter (and the rest of the apostles) had that right, so should he.

St. Peter and St. Paul share the same feast day, June 29.

STS. JOACHIM AND ANN

The Catholic Church celebrates the feast of Joachim and Ann (or Anne or Anna), the parents of Mary and the grandparents of Jesus, on July 26. However, nothing factual is known about them. We aren't even sure that their names were Joachim and Ann. Those names came from the *Protevangelium of James*, one of the many writings about Jesus that appeared after his death. The Church did not accept this writing as part of the New Testament, but that doesn't mean that all the facts in it were wrong. Many traditions about Mary and Joseph, now part of Catholic doctrine, also originated in the *Protevangelium of James*, as we will see in the chapter about Joseph and Mary.

The word "Protevangelium" means "initial gospel." It implies that the events recorded here occurred prior to those included in the Gospels that are part of the New Testament. However, the *Protevangelium of James* was written after the canonical Gospels. The earliest possible date for its composition is the middle of the second century and the latest possible date would be early in the third century since it was mentioned then by Origen. The most probable date is the middle of the second century, about 175 years after the events described occurred.

As is true of the canonical Gospels, this account used both oral and written sources. The stories included in this account were stories told by the earliest Christians.

Its authorship is attributed to James, identified as the stepbrother of Jesus, a matter that we'll discuss in the chapter about Mary and Joseph. It could not have actually been written by him, though, since he was martyred in the year 62.

Here, then, are the traditions about Joachim and Ann, the parents of Mary:

The very first line in the *Protevangelium of James* says, "In the 'Histories of the Twelve Tribes of Israel' Joachim was a very rich man." He and Ann lived in Jerusalem, near the Bethesda Pools. At that time, this part of town was located outside the city walls.

Joachim owned large flocks of sheep. He belonged to the royal kinship of the Davidids, those descended from King David. Ann was related to the lineage of the priests and was an older sister of Elizabeth, the mother of John the Baptist. This is how Elizabeth and Mary were related.

Joachim and Ann were childless and they were scorned by the Jews for that reason. Once when Joachim tried to offer gifts to God, he was told by a man named Reuben, "It is not fitting for you to offer your gifts because you have begotten no offspring in Israel." Feeling deeply offended, he took his flocks of sheep into the Judean wilderness where he fasted for 40 days and 40 nights.

Today the cave where it is believed Joachim lived during that time is at St. George Monastery, deep within the Wadi Kelt. It was there that he had a vision. An angel appeared to him and told him, "Joachim, Joachim, the Lord God has heard your prayer. Go down; behold, your wife Ann shall conceive." Joachim believed the angel and sacrificed 10 lambs without blemish, 12 calves and 100 kids. Then he went home to Ann.

Meanwhile, Ann was back in Jerusalem feeling just as sad about her barrenness as was Joachim. She went for a walk in the garden by her home and sat down under a laurel tree. She prayed, "O God of our fathers, bless me and hear my prayer, as you did bless the womb of Sarah and gave her a son, Isaac."

While she was lamenting her condition, an angel appeared to her and said, "Ann, Ann, the Lord has heard your prayer. You shall conceive and bear, and your offspring shall be spoken of in the whole world."

Ann then made this promise: "As the Lord my God lives, if I bear a child, whether male or female, I will bring it as a gift to the Lord my God, and it shall serve Him all the days of its life."

When Joachim arrived home, Ann was waiting for him at the gate and they both rejoiced over the messages each had received. There's a famous painting by Giotto in Padua's Arena Chapel showing this meeting.

And so Ann brought forth her child, probably around the year 25 B.C. The *Protevangelium* records: "And she said to the midwife: 'What have I brought forth?' And she said: 'A female.' And Ann said: 'My soul is magnified this day.' And she lay down. And when the days were fulfilled, Ann purified herself from her childbed and gave suck to the child, and called her Mary."

The writing also describes the great feast Joachim gave on Mary's first birthday: He "invited the chief priests and the scribes and the elders and the whole people of Israel." They blessed Mary saying, "O God of our fathers, bless this child and give her a name renowned for ever among all generations."

When Mary was two, Joachim suggested that it was time for them to present her in the Temple in accordance with the promise Ann made to present her child as a gift to God. This was similar to Hannah and Elkanah's child Samuel (cf. 1 Samuel 1:27-28), who also was considered a gift of God and who was presented in the Temple. (The name Ann derives from the Hebrew Hannah.) Ann, though, said, "Let us wait until the third year, that the child may then no more long after her father and mother." So Joachim agreed to wait.

When Mary was three, Joachim said, "Let us call the undefiled daughters of the Hebrews, and let each one take a lamp, and let these be burning, in order that the child may not turn back and her heart be enticed away from the Temple of the Lord." So they took Mary to the Temple and the priest received her. He said to Mary, "The Lord has magnified your name among all generations; because of you the Lord at the end of the days will manifest His redemption to the children of Israel."

Mary was happy to be in the Temple, "and the Lord God put grace upon the child, and she danced for joy with her feet, and the whole house of Israel loved her. And her parents went down wondering, praising and glorifying the almighty God because the child did not turn back to them. And Mary was in the Temple nurtured like a dove and received food from the hand of an angel."

That's the last we hear about Joachim and Ann. We have no idea when they died. Did they live long enough to know their grandson, Jesus? Did the Holy Family stay with them when they traveled from Nazareth to Jerusalem for the Jewish feasts? We simply don't know.

There is greater devotion to St. Ann today than there is to St. Joachim. The cult of St. Ann can be traced back as far as the 5th century in the East, but not in the West until the 13th century. A shrine in Douai, France was one of the early centers of the cult. In 1382 her feast was extended to the whole Western Church, and she became very popular, especially in France. Her most famous shrines are at St. Anne d'Auray in Brittany and St. Anne-de-Beaupre in Quebec, Canada. There are numerous paintings depicting Mary and St. Ann.

St. Ann is patroness of housewives and women in labor. She is also invoked by women who are looking for husbands.

STS. ZACHARY AND ELIZABETH

Everything we know about Sts. Zachary (or Zechariah) and Elizabeth comes from the Gospel According to Luke. They were the parents of John the Baptist, of whom Jesus himself said "among those born of women, no one is greater than John" (Luke 7:28).

Luke tells us that Zachary was of the priestly division of Abijah. This is the eighth of the 24 divisions of priests who, for a week at a time, twice a year, served in the Temple in Jerusalem. Elizabeth, his wife, was descended from the priestly line of Aaron, the brother of Moses. Luke says that she was a kinswoman of Mary but doesn't describe their relationship. Earliest traditions have it that she was a younger sister of Ann, Mary's mother, so she would have been Mary's aunt. They lived in the hill country of Judea, in Ein Karem, a suburb of Jerusalem.

We know that Zachary and Elizabeth (her name means "worshiper of God") were holy people who faithfully followed the Jewish commandments and ordinances. But, like Ann, Elizabeth was barren; she had no children and had reached the age when women are normally no longer fertile.

Then, one day Zachary was at the Temple performing his regular priestly duties. The priests in his division cast lots to see who would have the privilege of offering incense on the altar, and Zachary won. While he was alone inside the sanctuary, suddenly the angel Gabriel appeared to him, standing at the right of the altar. Zachary, naturally, was troubled, perhaps as much because an unauthorized man was in the sanctuary as anything else.

The angel told Zachary not to fear, a stereotyped Old Testament phrase spoken to reassure the recipient of a heavenly vision. Gabriel then told Zachary that the prayers of the priest and his wife would be answered and that a son would be born to them. Zachary found this hard to believe because, as he said, "I am an old man, and my wife is advanced in years." Because he doubted, the angel said that Zachary would be stricken dumb and would not be able to speak until his child was born.

The crowds outside the sanctuary were wondering what had happened to Zachary. When he finally came out, and could not speak, they realized that he had seen a vision.

Zachary went home and eventually Elizabeth did become pregnant, as the angel had said. As was customary, she went into seclusion, but she rejoiced that the Lord "has seen fit to take away my disgrace before others" (Luke 1:25). Barrenness was seen by the Jews at the time as punishment for sin.

Elizabeth was in the sixth month of her pregnancy when Mary came to visit her — a touching scene, known as the Visitation, that has been painted by many great artists. During the Annunciation, when Mary was told that she would conceive Jesus, she had also been told that Elizabeth had conceived and was then in her sixth month.

Miraculous things occurred when Mary, pregnant with Jesus, greeted Elizabeth. First, as Elizabeth told her, "the infant in my womb leaped for joy" at the presence of Jesus (Luke 1:44). The Church has taught that this was a sign that John had been cleansed of original sin and would have the privilege of being born without original sin. (Only Jesus and Mary were *conceived* without original sin.) This fulfilled the promise made to Zachary by the angel Gabriel, who said about John, "He will be filled with the Holy Spirit even from his mother's womb" (1:15).

Then Elizabeth herself was cleansed from original sin since Luke says that she was filled with the Holy Spirit. She cried out to Mary, "Most blessed are you among women and blessed is the fruit of your womb. And how does this happen to me, that the mother of my Lord should come to me? For at the moment the sound of your greeting reached my ears, the infant in my womb leaped for joy. Blessed are you who believed that what was spoken to you by the Lord would be fulfilled" (Luke 1:42-45).

Mary remained with Elizabeth for three months, but Luke doesn't say she was there during John's birth. However, it would be strange for her to stay with Elizabeth up to the time the birth was imminent and then leave. So it's probable that she was present during John's birth.

When John was born, Elizabeth's neighbors all rejoiced with her. When the baby was ready to be circumcised on the eighth day after his birth, relatives and friends expected him to be named after his father. They were taken by surprise when Elizabeth announced that his name was going to be John. They even argued with her, pointing out that no one in the family had that name. Finally, they appealed to Zachary to see what the father wanted to name him.

Zachary signaled for a writing tablet and wrote simply, "John is his name." Immediately the punishment for doubting the words of Gabriel was lifted and Zachary regained his speech. He praised God and recited the Canticle of Zechariah that the Church includes every day in Morning Prayer in the Liturgy of the Hours. As part of this canticle, he said, "And you, my child, will be called the prophet of the Most High, for you will go before the Lord to prepare His way, to give His people knowledge of salvation through the forgiveness of sins" (Luke 1:76-77).

We know nothing more about Zachary and Elizabeth. They obviously raised their son in accordance with the instructions given to Zachary by Gabriel: "He will drink neither wine nor strong drink" (Luke 1:15). Luke says that "John grew and became strong in spirit, and he was in the desert until the day of his manifestation to Israel" (1:80).

The Church observes the feast of Sts. Zachary and Elizabeth on November 5.

STS. MARY AND JOSEPH

Certainly the most important married saints are Mary and Joseph, the mother and foster father of Jesus. Unfortunately, we don't know as much about these two saints as we would like to know.

We know a little more about Mary than we know about Joseph, but not much more. She appears in all four Gospels, but is mentioned by name only in Matthew and Luke. In Mark there's the episode where Jesus' mother and brothers arrive outside. When he is told they are there, Jesus asks, "Who are my mother and brothers? Whoever does the will of God is my brother and sister and mother." That's Mark's only mention of Mary and he doesn't mention Joseph at all.

John's Gospel's treatment of Mary is puzzling. He tells us that, while Jesus was hanging on the cross, he entrusted Mary to "the disciple Jesus loved" (always assumed to be John) and that "from that hour the disciple took her into his home." Yet nowhere in John's Gospel does he tell us what

Jesus' mother's name was. The only other mention of Mary in John's Gospel was at the marriage feast at Cana where Jesus performed his first miracle at his mother's request. In both instances, Jesus addresses his mother as "woman," as in "Woman, behold your son" and "Woman, how does your concern affect me? My hour has not yet come." If Mary lived with John after Jesus' death, why wouldn't he have been the one to tell us about Jesus' birth since Mary could have told him about it? Instead, the infancy narratives come from men who, so far as we know, never had any connection with Mary.

Much of what the Church has come to accept about Mary is not in the Gospels but in what was eventually declared to be an apocryphal account — the *Protevangelium of James*. There are more than 15 non-canonical accounts of the life of Jesus, including the *Infancy Gospel of Thomas*, the *Arabic Gospel of the Infancy*, the *History of Joseph the Carpenter*, the *Acts of John*, *Acts of Peter*, and *Acts of Andrew*. The early Church decided that none of them were divinely inspired. However, that doesn't mean that everything in them was wrong.

As we have already seen, in the chapter about Sts. Joachim and Ann, it was from the *Protevangelium of James* that we learned that these were the names of Mary's parents. According to tradition, they lived in Jerusalem, right by the Pool of

Bethesda. Today the Church of St. Anne is there. Pilgrims to the Holy Land can walk down to the crypt of the church to what is claimed to be the site of Mary's birth, which occurred in about the year 25 B.C.

Catholic tradition, and the apocryphal *Prote vangelium of James*, also claims that Mary was presented to the Temple by her parents when she was three years old, in thanksgiving for her birth after they had been barren for many years. And somewhere along the line Mary decided to remain a virgin all her life.

According to Luke's Gospel, the angel Gabriel appeared to Mary in Nazareth. So when did she move there? We have no idea. Supposedly she lived in the Temple until it was time for her to be betrothed. Did she go back to live with her parents, and did they then move to Nazareth? It seems unlikely but it's even more unlikely that a teenage girl would have moved there by herself.

This is where we get into differences in the Gospel accounts. Let's follow each one, Luke's first.

According to Luke, Mary was living in Nazareth where she was betrothed to Joseph. Betrothal was the first part of the marriage process for Jews. It was more than an engagement period because it constituted a man and woman as husband and wife and subsequent infidelity was considered adultery. The betrothal was followed some months later by the husband's taking his wife into his home, at which time normal married life began.

Anyway, the angel appears to Mary and tells her that she has been selected to be the mother of the Son of the Most High. We then learn that she intends to remain a virgin when she asks how this could happen and we learn that it will happen when the Holy Spirit comes upon her. She is also told that her relative Elizabeth is pregnant. She accepts the angel's word, consents to the plan, and becomes pregnant.

Now, I've passed over the Annunciation fairly quickly, which I really shouldn't do because I think there is more Catholic theology in Luke 1:26-38 than in any New Testament passage except the prologue to John's Gospel. For example, the only biblical allusion to the doctrine of the Immaculate Conception (that Mary was conceived without original sin) is the angel's greeting, "Hail, full of grace" (or "favored one" or "highly favored one," depending upon the translation). Nobody could be full of grace if he or she had original sin on his or her soul and the fact that Mary didn't made her "highly favored." Other doctrines in this passage include the existence of angels and their mission, the virgin birth of Jesus, and, in verse 35, the existence of the entire Trinity (the Holy Spirit, the Most High and the Son of God). The Jews only knew about one God and didn't know about the three persons, but the angel mentions them to Mary.

Luke then tells us that Mary traveled "in haste" to a town of Judah to visit Elizabeth. It couldn't have been in too much of a haste because the trip from Nazareth in Galilee to Ein Karem in Judea was not an easy trip. It wasn't a matter of jumping in a car and driving for an hour-and-a-half. A young girl couldn't possibly have made the trip by herself. She would have had to go in a caravan, and certainly with a chaperon, and the trip would have taken her about a week, down along the Jordan River to Jericho and then up to Jerusalem and then to Ein Karem. She sure had a lot of faith in Gabriel's word to make such a trip. What if she had arrived and congratulated Elizabeth on her pregnancy and had Elizabeth say, "What are you talking about? Are you crazy?"

Instead, we get another grace-filled story: When Mary comes into the presence of John in the womb, he is cleansed of original sin and leaps for joy. Then Elizabeth is cleansed of original sin and is filled with the Holy Spirit. The infant Jesus is performing acts of redemption even before his birth. St. Jerome wrote about these cleansings of original sin at the time of the Visitation. John was the second person to be born without original sin, but only Mary and Jesus were *conceived* without original sin.

Luke says that Mary remained with Elizabeth for three months. Since Gabriel told Mary that Elizabeth was in her sixth month, Mary was apparently with Elizabeth when John was born. Then, Luke says, she returned home. But Luke never tells us when Mary told Joseph that she was pregnant. Was this a big surprise when Mary went back to Nazareth? Matthew tells us that Joseph decided to divorce Mary quietly, but Luke is silent about the matter. In Luke's story, Joseph's betrothed went away for three months and, when she returned, she was pregnant. But Luke makes no mention of Joseph's feelings at all.

Well, the *Protevangelium of James* does. It describes the confrontation Joseph had with Mary when he came to take her to his home and saw that she was pregnant. In that account, though, Joseph first blames himself for not protecting Mary: "For I received her as a virgin out of the Temple of the Lord my God and have not protected her." Then, just as in Matthew's account, Joseph has a dream in which he learns that she has conceived by the Holy Spirit. Then they both face the high priest, who accuses both of them and they have to convince him that they have not had sexual relations.

Now we return to Luke. He then jumps ahead to the birth of Jesus and the reasons why Mary and Joseph go to Bethlehem, a trip that was about the same distance as when Mary went to Ein Karem since both towns are suburbs of Jerusalem. One thing that's surprising about Luke's account is that he says that Joseph went to Bethlehem with Mary, "his betrothed" or "espoused wife." He doesn't say just "his wife." Hadn't they begun to live together yet? Luke isn't clear about that.

So Mary has her baby. Many women through the centuries have prayed to Mary at the time of their childbirth, thinking that Mary understood the pains of childbirth. The Church teaches that that was not the case. Since Mary was conceived without original sin, she did not have to undergo the curse that God imposed on humans after Adam and Eve sinned. God said to Eve, "I will intensify the pangs of your childbearing; in pain shall you bring forth children" (Genesis 3:16). But that wasn't true for Mary.

Besides, the Catholic Church has always taught that Mary was a virgin "before, during and after the birth of Jesus." We know what before and after the birth of Jesus means, but we seldom think about the meaning of "during." The Church means that, during the birth, Mary remained physically intact, that her hymen wasn't broken. Thus Pope Leo the Great wrote in his *Tome*: "(Mary) brought him forth without the loss of virginity, even as she conceived him without the loss of virginity. It was a miraculous birth." And St. Augustine wrote: "A virgin who conceives, a virgin who gives birth; a virgin with Child, a virgin delivered of Child, a virgin ever virgin! Why do you marvel at these things, O man? When God vouchsafed to become man, it was fitting that he should be born in this way."

And where did the tradition of Mary's virginity during birth come from? Again, from the *Protevangelium of James*. It describes a scene where, in the cave, "a great light appeared, so that our eyes could not bear it. A short time afterwards that light withdrew until the child appeared." Then it tells about a midwife who meets another midwife named Salome and tells her, "Salome, Salome, I have a new sight to tell you; a virgin has brought forth, a thing which her nature does not allow." And Salome said: "As the Lord my God lives, unless I put forward my finger and test her condition, I will not believe that a virgin has brought forth." She then goes into the cave and tests her condition.

We are all familiar with the rest of Luke's story after Jesus' birth (the worship by the shepherds, the circumcision, the presentation in the Temple, and finally the peaceful return to Nazareth, where the Holy Family lived until it was time for Jesus to begin his public life).

But Matthew tells us a completely different story. Matthew has Mary and Joseph living in Bethlehem, not in Nazareth. When Mary is found to be with child, Joseph is perplexed, to say the least. Here was a terrible dilemma, especially since the Jewish penalty for adultery was death by stoning. Matthew agrees with Luke that the couple were betrothed but not yet living together, and he also agrees with Luke that the child was conceived by the Holy Spirit. Matthew tells us that an angel tells Joseph this in a dream and, therefore, he took Mary into his home. So there is no doubt in Matthew's Gospel that they were married. There is also no doubt in Matthew's Gospel that Mary was still a virgin until she bore a son, although he is silent about what happened during and after the birth.

After the birth, though, we get a completely different story than we had in Luke's Gospel. We learn from Matthew that magi appeared in Jerusalem and talked with King Herod. If this is true, then Jesus had to have been born earlier than we usually think of his birth because Herod the Great ruled from 37 B.C. to 4 B.C. Today many historians and biblical scholars believe Jesus was born about the year 7 B.C. and died in 30 A.D., so he was probably about four years older during his public life than we were taught as we were growing up.

So Matthew tells us about the visit of the magi and the treachery of King Herod. He tells us that Joseph took Mary and Jesus to Egypt in order to escape from Herod and so that the Scripture passage from Hosea could be fulfilled: "Out of Egypt I called my son." They stayed in Egypt until Herod died. Then Joseph returned to Palestine. But when he learned that Herod's son, Archelaus, was ruling over Judea, Matthew says that he was afraid to return to Bethlehem. Instead they traveled to Galilee and made their home in Nazareth.

So Luke and Matthew told different stories. But they agree that Jesus was born in Bethlehem and grew up in Nazareth. As for Mary, if she lived in Bethlehem instead of Nazareth at the time of her marriage, she would have been much closer to her birthplace of Jerusalem, and, of course, to the Temple where tradition and the *Protevangelium of James* say she lived. We simply don't know whether Luke's Gospel is correct or if Matthew's is.

Wherever Mary and Joseph lived prior to Jesus' birth, we know that Nazareth was Mary's home during the following 30 years or so. Both Luke and Matthew agree on that.

One of the sites pointed out to tourists and pilgrims to Nazareth today is Mary's well. A Greek Orthodox church is built over the well and pilgrims still get water from it. There is every reason to believe that it was the well used by Mary to get water for the family (for drinking, bathing, washing of clothes and dishes, etc.). Just as today many Palestinians still travel daily to wells in towns of Galilee or on the West Bank, that's what all women had to do back when Mary lived. The well was about 500 yards outside of town when the Holy Family lived there.

In Nazareth, too, the most important shrine is the Church of the Annunciation, with its grotto. This is believed to be the site of the Annunciation, if Luke's account is accurate. Almost next door is the Church of St. Joseph with its excavations. Today pilgrims walk above deep pits where the home of the Holy Family is believed to have been. Since only about 120 to 150 people lived in the village of Nazareth at the time of Christ, the entire town is under those churches.

Joseph supported his family through his occupation as a carpenter. Actually, he was more than a carpenter. The Gospels use the word *tekton*, which is a master builder, somebody who worked on the various materials needed for construction work, including timber and iron, but most frequently stone. Since there is so much stone in the Holy Land, most homes and other buildings are built with stone.

Since Nazareth was such a small village, it's probable that Joseph (and later, Jesus) did construction work in Sepphoris, about an hour's walk from Nazareth. Sepphoris was the capital of Galilee at the time and a much larger city than Nazareth.

The Gospels tell us only one story about the Holy Family while Jesus was growing up but we can learn quite a bit from that story. Luke says that they used to go to Jerusalem for Passover every year, which indicates that they were a religious family — something we would naturally assume. At the end of the observance the year that Jesus was 12, Mary and Joseph were returning to Nazareth and had gone a day's journey before they realized that Jesus was not with them. So they returned to Jerusalem and found Jesus in the Temple.

How was it possible for them to go a day's journey without knowing that Jesus was missing? It was customary in caravans for the men to travel together and the women to travel with the children. Since Jesus was 12, Mary probably assumed that he was with the men and Joseph assumed that he was with the women. At the end of the day, they realized that that was not so. Therefore, after looking for him among their relatives and friends, the next day they returned to Jerusalem and, on the following day, found Jesus in the Temple. Parents can imagine the anxiety and worry Joseph and Mary must have felt.

At some point, Mary became a widow; nobody knows when. Widows at that time usually had to have a man take care of them since there weren't income-producing jobs for women. We assume that she was cared for by Jesus, but perhaps by stepsons. (Or perhaps she inherited Joachim's wealth.) The Gospels and the Acts of the Apostles refer to Jesus' brothers and this has always been a problem for the Church, since it insists on Mary's perpetual virginity. Usually it is assumed that Jesus' brothers were actually cousins or some other relatives, but there is also the thought within the Church that they might have been Joseph's children by a previous marriage. This is the earliest tradition and is still believed by the Orthodox Church.

And where does that come from? From the *Protevangelium of James*, of course. It is quite clear in its story of the betrothal of Mary and Joseph. It tells the story of the priests in the Temple trying to figure out what to do with Mary: "Behold," they say, "Mary has become 12 years old in the Temple of the Lord. What then shall we do with her, that she may not pollute the Temple of the Lord?" (In other words, they had to get her out of the Temple before she started to menstruate, at which time, according to Judaism, she would be ritually unclean and could not be in the Temple.)

It then goes on to describe how widowers were assembled, and Joseph was one of them. A dove came out of Joseph's rod and flew onto his head, so the high priest told him that to him had fallen the good fortune to receive Mary and "take her under your care." Joseph protests that "I already have sons and am old," but finally agrees to take Mary as his wife. This is where we get the idea that Joseph was much older than Mary.

The *Protevangelium* also says that Joseph's sons went with him and Mary to Bethlehem to be registered and, when they arrived, "he left Mary in the care of his sons and went out to seek for a Hebrew midwife in the region of Bethlehem." More evidence that Joseph had children who became Mary's stepchildren.

There is, by the way, a discrepancy in this story of Mary. The priests say that Mary is 12 when a husband is chosen for her, but at the time of the Annunciation and Visitation, the *Protevangelium* says, "And Mary was 16 years old when all these mysterious things happened."

The *Protevangelium* also has this passage: "Now there went out a decree from the king Augustus that all inhabitants of Bethlehem in Judaea should be enrolled. And Joseph said, 'I shall enroll my sons, but what shall I do with this child? How shall I enroll her? As my wife? I am ashamed to do that. Or as my daughter? But all the children of Israel know that she is not my daughter.'" It's a curious passage. Why was Joseph ashamed to enroll Mary as his wife? It must be because of the great difference in their ages, especially since Mary was still a teenager. Apparently Joseph thought of Mary more as a daughter than as a wife, which, of course, would explain his willingness to accept the fact that Mary wanted to remain a virgin.

After Jesus began his public life, there is nothing to indicate that Mary traveled with him. She apparently stayed home in Nazareth when Jesus moved to Capernaum, except for the one time when she "and his brothers" arrived at Capernaum to see him. The Gospels tell us that some women accompanied Jesus and the apostles. They were led by Mary Magdalene, and others mentioned were Joanna and Susanna. The mother of James and John also was among the women because, during one trip, she approached Jesus and asked for special places for her sons when Jesus came into his kingdom. These women "provided for them out of their resources" (Luke 8:3) and they undoubtedly also did the cooking and the laundry. But there is no mention that Mary was among the women. If she was, you'd think it would be mentioned.

Yet, according to John, Mary was present when Jesus was crucified. John is the only evangelist to say that Jesus' mother was there, apparently to indicate that this was when Jesus entrusted her to him. If Mary wasn't among the women who usually traveled with Jesus, how did she get to the site of the crucifixion? This is only speculation on my part, but I think the answer is in Luke's Gospel where he tells about the 12-year old Jesus lost and then found in the Temple. He starts that story by saying that each year Mary and Joseph went to Jerusalem for the feast of Passover. Well, Jesus was crucified during the time of the Passover, so I've always thought that Mary was in Jerusalem for that feast.

At the time of the crucifixion, I visualize someone running to wherever Mary was staying to tell her that her son has been arrested and is going to be crucified. She arrives along the route where Jesus is carrying the cross (where, in the Way of the Cross, Jesus meets his mother). The anguish they both felt had to have been intense.

After Jesus' resurrection, tradition says that

he appeared first to his mother. That's not in the Bible anyplace, and we don't have to believe it, but St. Ignatius of Loyola taught it. Furthermore, there's a chapel in the Church of the Holy Sepulchre (the largest private chapel in the church) called the Apparition Chapel, built where Jesus is supposed to have appeared to Mary. However, my belief is that, if Jesus did appear to his mother, it was probably somewhere else in Jerusalem since there is no evidence that Mary was near the tomb on the first Easter.

After Jesus ascended to heaven, the Acts of the Apostles tells us that Mary was present with the apostles in the upper room. She was probably there on Pentecost. Then she drops out of the Scriptures. What happened to her after that?

There is a place in Ephesus, in modern Turkey, where, it is claimed, Mary lived with the apostle John. The Ephesians believe that Mary died in Ephesus and was buried there before she was assumed into heaven. However, in Jerusalem the Church of the Dormition (which is a Benedictine Abbey) is located at the top of Mount Zion. It is believed that Mary died there. There is also the Tomb of Mary located next to the Garden of Gethsemane. It is believed that Mary was buried there and was then assumed into heaven.

I favor Jerusalem. If John went to Ephesus I think it had to have been after Mary died. We know from Acts that Paul lived in Ephesus for two years and there is no indication that Mary and John were there at that time. If they had been, certainly Luke would have mentioned it since Luke, the author of Acts, was the one who wrote most about Mary in his Gospel. And in Paul's Letter to the Ephesians there is no indication that Mary or John is in that city. So it's my opinion that Mary continued to live in Jerusalem and died there. Tradition says she died at age 70.

After her death, of course, we believe that she was assumed into heaven where she was crowned Queen of Heaven and Earth. She has continued to make appearances on earth as she encourages us to live holy lives, and she intercedes for us with God in heaven. So also, of course, does her husband, St. Joseph.